The Prayer Life

YOU'VE ALWAYS WANTED

You're Only as Strong as
Your Prayer Life

THOMAS J. RAMUNDO

WESTBOW
P R E S S®
A DIVISION OF THOMAS NELSON
& ZONDERVAN

WestBow Press books may be ordered through booksellers or by contacting:

WestBow Press
A Division of Thomas Nelson & Zondervan
1663 Liberty Drive
Bloomington, IN 47403
www.westbowpress.com
844-714-3454

ISBN: 978-1-6642-2013-3 (sc)
ISBN: 978-1-6642-2014-0 (hc)
ISBN: 978-1-6642-2015-7 (e)

Library of Congress Control Number: 2021901511

Print information available on the last page.

WestBow Press rev. date: 02/24/2021

Life's most wonderful privilege is conversation with God. This is the Christian's birthright, along with the promise that God hears and answers prayer.
—Harold Lindsell

This book is dedicated to the glory of God.

In memory of my grandmother, Theresa Orrico Casurella, who, every day after lunch, closed her bedroom door and in her native Italian language prayed passionately. Sometimes you could hear her all over the house, and on summer days with the windows open, she could be heard out in the yard too. While I didn't always understand what she was saying, I could tell that she meant it and that she was sure God was listening. And since I recognized my name in Italian, I knew I was the subject of many of those prayers.

In memory of my mother, Mary Casurella Ramundo, whose prayers, along with those of my father, lay a firm foundation for a home in which they raised three sons to know and serve the Lord. At the age of fifteen I gave my heart to the Lord after overhearing Mom praying fervently and tearfully for me to come to faith in Christ. Another reason to dedicate this book to my mother is that for years she hounded me to write it. Well, Mom, here it is. Finally.

In honor of my wife, Noni Graz Ramundo, for over half a century my partner in life, ministry, and prayer, whose indefatigable intercessory efforts on my behalf and by my side have meant the world to me, our family, countless individuals, and the kingdom of God. And when it comes to this book, as has been true in my more than fifty years of preaching, her input has been of inestimable value.

In honor of my daughters, Theresa Marie Anderson and Christy May Davis: Growing up in our home, they were a part of our many adventures in life, ministry, and prayer. They are strong women of faith, and I could not be prouder of them.

CONTENTS

ACKNOWLEDGMENTS

In addition to my wife and daughters, along with my mother and grandmother, to whom this book is dedicated, there are others I would like to recognize.

My late father, Thomas Ramundo Sr., modelled for me a faithful daily time in the Word and prayer.

I am grateful for the influence of two individuals now in heaven who appear in these pages: Ernest Kratzer, pastor of the church of my childhood, and Jennie Master, member of a church I pastored. The memory of their Christlike living and commitment to prayer continues to be an inspiration to me.

I also want to give a tip of the hat to these individuals whose stories I share: Ron Burley, Doug Campbell, Pastor Steve Glei, and Mike and Connie MacGuinness.

I give a shout out to the people of the Jackson, Michigan, Free Methodist Church, especially Warren Hawkins and Judy Osborne, along with two ladies now with the Lord, Gladys Langhern and Evelyn Lewandowski. Faithful participants in the Prayer Force, they loved and encouraged me as we experienced together the joy of a church growing spiritually, as well as in numbers and influence, through the power of prayer.

I am indebted to several teachers, preachers, authors, and friends, past and present, whose spoken and written ministries in the Word have directed and deepened my appreciation, understanding, personal practice, and teaching of prayer: E. M. Bounds, Jim Cymbala, Wesley Duewel, Ben Haden, K. C. Hairston, Bruce Hildenbrand, Harold Lindsell, Peter Marshall, D. L. Moody, Darrell Moore, George Mueller, Stormie Omartian, Elmer Parsons, Leonard Ravenhill, Charles Spurgeon, Corrie Ten Boom, and Ralph Thompson.

I owe a great debt of gratitude to two individuals who read my manuscript, giving me valuable feedback, encouragement, corrections, and suggestions. Linda Hass has forty years of experience writing for daily newspapers and regional magazines, and has authored three books. Charles White is a Bible scholar, theologian, and professor of Christian Thought and History at Spring Arbor University, who has two books to his credit, along with numerous scholarly articles and scores of popular essays.

Finally, I want to recognize Natalie Anderson, a publishing and marketing student at Cornerstone University. Natalie, who is completing her junior year, was instrumental in helping me whip my manuscript into final shape. I found the many hours we spent working together a joy, as they should have been. After all, she's my granddaughter.

PREFACE

The Prayer Life You've Always Wanted

Why a book on the prayer life you've always wanted? Because while every follower of Christ recognizes the importance and value of a consistent and vital prayer life, many struggle to succeed in this essential aspect of Christian living. Even seasoned saints, who have witnessed the wonder and power of prayer for a lifetime, often feel they fall far short of experiencing the full potential of prayer.

Pastor and religious broadcaster Ben Haden no doubt mirrored the feelings of many believers when he came on the air one time and began his message saying, "Since becoming a believer in Christ, I've had a two-bit prayer life, and nothing has troubled me more. And yet I have every reason, perhaps just like you, not to have a two-bit prayer life."

When I served on the editorial board of a Christian publication, from time to time we would survey our readership to ascertain what topics they would like to see addressed in the magazine. We wanted to know what they felt would be most helpful to them. And every time we conducted such a survey, prayer, by far, was at the top of the list. Our readers' most pressing need was the need to learn more about prayer and how to have a strong, effective, consistent prayer life.

If you are among those who desire to grow in conversation and communion with the Lord, this book is for you and comes with the sincere hope it will assist you in the pursuit of the prayer life you've always wanted.

In these pages we will explore biblical teaching on the

principles, privileges, and promises of prayer, along with practical applications, and all served up with an ample supply of real-life stories to illustrate and motivate. At the same time, I have not shied away from dealing with some of the difficult questions that arise when our prayers don't seem to be producing the results we are looking for.

I believe prayer is the greatest adventure of the Christian life, and it is my hope that you, if you don't already, will come to know it that way too.

Yours for the prayer life you've always wanted,
Thomas

INTRODUCTION

You Are Only as Strong
as Your Prayer Life

"The main thing is to keep the main thing the main thing." Those words, catchy and clever to be sure, can be seen on bumper stickers, heard at seminars and conferences, and found in leadership books. It is my firm conviction that for everybody who's a believer and for every body of believers, the main thing is prayer, or at least it ought to be. "Too simplistic," you say. "An exaggeration." I don't think so. What good is anything we do in Christian living and serving if not bathed in prayer before, during, and after doing it? Author and evangelical minister Samuel Dickey Gordon said, "You can do more than pray after you have prayed, but you cannot do more than pray until you have prayed."

Others agree prayer is the main thing. Evangelist and religious radio pioneer Fred Francis Bosworth wrote, "Prayer isn't another iron in the fire; it is the fire." Author Edward McKendree Bounds tells us, "Prayer is not preparation for the battle, prayer is the battle." Oswald Chambers, best known for his devotional book, *My Utmost for His Highest,* adds, "Prayer does not equip us for greater works; prayer is the greater work."

The purpose of this book is to explore and explain principles, practices, and even some problems of life-breathing, growth-producing, strength-imparting, grace-releasing, miracle-unleashing, kingdom-building, God-honoring prayer.

What I have to share grows out of a lifetime of observation, study, experience, and fascination with the subject of prayer, all of which brought me a long time ago to conclude *you are only as strong as your prayer life*. It has been observed that if you are not a praying person, you must carry your faith. But if you are a praying person, your faith carries you. Yes, prayer is just that critical to spiritual life, health, and growth.

The Old Testament's Daniel, known and lauded for his strength of character and uncompromising stand for God, knelt and prayed three times a day.[1] Daniel was strong because his prayer life was strong.

Hebrews 4:14–16, one of the Bible's classic passages on prayer, is the focus and foundation for our exploration into prayer in this book:

> So then, since we have a great High Priest who has entered heaven, Jesus the Son of God, let us hold firmly to what we believe. This High Priest of ours understands our weaknesses, for he faced all of the same testings we do, yet he did not sin. So let us come boldly to the throne of our gracious God. There we will receive his mercy, and we will find grace to help us when we need it most.

Those three verses give us the confidence that when we pray, God is rooting for us and all heaven is cheering us on. And when you dovetail those verses with those that immediately precede them, along with other scriptures on prayer, the cheering rises to a roar.

It is my hope and prayer that this book will help you be prayer strong and give you instruction and inspiration enough to take you more often and more "boldly to the throne of our gracious God." After all, when it comes to prayer, God is stacking the deck in our favor. Because of his graciousness, we experience, as the title of the old hymn suggests, both the "Sweet Hour of Prayer" and the sweet power of prayer.

---

[1] Daniel 6:10.

I was raised in a home where prayer was prominent and practiced, and I have always been a part of churches that took prayer seriously. My greatest joys in living and serving have either been in prayer or because of prayer. Throughout our marriage, my wife, Noni, and I have endeavored to make prayer a key component of our relationship. We take great pleasure in coming together daily before the throne of grace, a practice we began while dating back in our student days. I relish teaching and preaching on prayer and enjoy leading Prayer Warrior Boot Camp, a weekend event at churches and in other settings.

I heard about a Christian publisher who contacted a well-known evangelical pastor and author to ask him to write a book on prayer. The pastor declined, saying that while he believed strongly in prayer and faithfully practiced it, he felt he had a long way to go before he was worthy of writing a book about it. The publisher moved on to another well-known Christian leader, and then a third, each in turn giving the same reply as the first!

Even though those three were well-respected elder statesmen in the faith with lifetimes of walking with the Lord and renowned service to the church, they still felt they were beginners in the school of prayer. Prayer is something even the most ardent follower of Christ can never completely comprehend, let alone clearly communicate. You will understand, then, when I say it is with more than a little humility I have undertaken this effort. But it is with the sincere desire the result will be more believers who are prayer strong. After all, you're only as strong as your prayer life.

The Grace of God Inviting Us

So let us come boldly to the throne of our gracious God. There we will receive his mercy, and we will find grace to help us when we need it most.

HEBREWS 4:16

People started suspecting I'd be a minister when I was in third grade. That's when I led my first prayer meeting. It happened one year before Madalyn Murray O'Hair and the United States Supreme Court decided that prayer—what President George Washington knelt to do in the snows of Valley Forge to help get America started and President Abraham Lincoln knelt to do in the White House to help keep America together—was unacceptable to do in school to help keep America going.

Near the end of a school day in a third-grade classroom at suburban Chicago Stevenson Elementary School, our teacher, Mrs. Ford, discovered someone had swiped something from her desk. I can't remember what was taken, but the teacher was clear. Either the culprit would confess, or we would all stay after school until…

Until? Until what? She never said, but we knew it couldn't be good. And when the little felon did not fess up, she left us alone to figure it out. She marched to the hall, high heels clicking on the floor. Yes, there was a time teachers wore high heels to school. The door closed gently behind her. In silence we sat, pondering our plight.

A few moments passed, and then trembling I rose to my feet and informed the class that if we came home late because we had been kept after school, our parents might kill us. Lest you think I exaggerate, you need to know this happened in one of Chicagoland's "Little Italy" neighborhoods, so the threat of homicide was never far from our minds. "There's only one thing to do," I counseled the class, drawing upon my upbringing in church world, "and that's pray." I then suggested we get down on our knees, just like I'd seen the grown-ups do at church on prayer meeting night, and enlist the aid of the Almighty.

We knelt, I led out in prayer, and I can only imagine what Mrs. Ford must have thought when, a few minutes later, she reentered the room, greeted by the sight of twenty-some nine-year-olds down on their knees next to their desks, crying and pouring out their hearts in search of divine intervention. So moved was this dear woman by the sight of all these repentant sinners prostrate on the school room floor, she took pity, granted us clemency, commuted our sentence, and set us free from the valley of the shadow of death. Our prayers had been answered.

In case you're wondering if the thief was ever brought to justice, the answer is no. He or she skated free, no doubt to embark upon a life of crime.

I don't know if that third-grade experience is what convinced me of the power of prayer, but it was at the very least a start, my first toddling steps in the direction of prayer's primacy in my walk with and work for the Lord. Evangelism and preaching, two activities that never fail to light a fire of passion in me, are at best tied for second compared to the place prayer holds in my heart. Besides, where would evangelism and preaching be without prayer?

2

By the way, had we been in third-grade *after* the Supreme Court banned school prayer, would we have prayed anyway? You bet. Desperate times call for desperate measures. Even third graders know that.

Come Boldly to the King's Throne

In some meager way, that fateful third grade day was my first experience doing what Hebrews 4:16 invites us to do—to "come boldly to the throne of our gracious God. There we will receive his mercy, and we will find grace to help us when we need it most." What a compelling invitation to intercession. It makes it clear that God's grace is at once the catalyst for our prayers and the answer to them. And with welcoming words like that, why would we ever hesitate to pray? And how could we ever feel we are a nuisance to the Almighty? Nineteenth-century evangelist Dwight L. Moody observed, "Some people think God does not like to be troubled with our constant coming and asking, but the only way to trouble God is not to come at all."

In Hebrews 4:16 the God of grace and the grace of God invite us to approach him *boldly*. Some Bibles translate "boldly" as "bravely" or "fearlessly," and still others render it "with confidence" or "confidently." Make no mistake about it, this scripture is no invitation to lily-livered, Mickey Mouse, half-baked, wimpy prayer. We're not just invited to come—were invited to come *boldly* to the throne of our gracious God in search of grace.

French King Louis XIV moved the capital from Paris to the Palace of Versailles in 1682, where it remained through the reigns of his two successors until 1789. Surrounded by lush gardens, the centerpiece of the outlandish seven-hundred-room palace was the opulent Hall of Mirrors with 357 floor-to-ceiling gold-framed mirrors. When visitors to the court, including emissaries of foreign governments and heads of state approached the king, they had to stop several times to curtsy as they made their way up the hall's 241-foot-long aisle to the dazzling silver throne on which Louis sat! The monarch, who dubbed himself "The Sun King," known for his gargantuan ego and sensuous excesses, instituted this practice so those who came before him would do so in recognition of his greatness, power, and glory.

We too have a King; one who far surpasses any earthly ruler in majesty and might. Our King is the divine designer of the star-spangled night who spun our sun and solar system into place in space in a universe of two trillion galaxies. He is the maker of our planet, and everything in it, and everyone on it. And we have an invitation from our King, the eternal God, to freely and confidently come before his throne, anytime night or day, no ingratiating groveling required.

Our King—sovereign creator and ruler of the universe—is infinitely powerful and at the same time intimately personal. Our King is great, yet gracious. He is tremendously awesome, yet tenderly approachable. He's not only mighty God, he's mighty good. Thus, we may approach his throne with our petitions freely, not fearfully, in confidence and boldness. And he bids us to do so unceasingly.[2]

Since the welcome mat is out, we should turn up on his doorstep as often as he wishes we would, especially since prayer is beyond important—it is essential. If it were merely important, it would be good to partake of it most of the time and OK to leave it some of the time. Since it is essential, however, we can't get along without it any of the time. No wonder Dutch author and humanitarian Corrie Ten Boom confronts you and me with the probing question, "Is prayer your spare tire or your steering wheel?" When it's your spare tire, it's just something you haul out in case of an emergency. The rest of the time it just sits there, mostly forgotten. But when it's your steering wheel, it is

---

[2] 1 Thessalonians 5:17.

indispensable. It sets the course of your direction and every move you make, everywhere you go. It guides you through every twist and turn on the highway of life.

God Invented Prayer

Prayer was God's idea in the first place. He invented it. It's pretty important to him. It must be, or he wouldn't have put so much of it in the Bible. The Bible is full of prayers, of calls to prayer, of reasons to pray, of instructions on praying, of stories of people praying, and of God answering their prayers. There's even a verse in Proverbs that says a believer praying brings delight to the heart of God.[3] Imagine that! And a verse in James tells us the sincere prayer of a godly person packs a wallop and yields remarkable results.[4]

The Bible contains more than 850 separate references to prayer. It includes the wording of some 650 specific prayers. No less than 450 of those prayers have recorded answers of how prayer changed lives, bestowed blessings, and guided believers. They tell the story of how prayer freed slaves, cured illnesses, and restored relationships. They relate how prayer unleashed love and grace, brought solace to the sorrowing and hope to the hopeless, altered the direction of nations, and shaped the course of human history.

In the Old Testament, patriarch Abraham prayed, and God demonstrated his love for the lost. Lawgiver Moses prayed, and God spared Israel from judgment. Military leader Joshua prayed, and the sun stood still. Infertile Hannah prayed, and God gave her a baby boy. Wealthy King Solomon prayed, and God gave him wisdom. Prayer warrior Elijah prayed, and fire

---

[3] Proverbs 15:8.
[4] James 5:16.

fell from Heaven, consuming a sacrifice on the altar. Elijah's successor Elisha prayed, and God gave him a double portion of the Spirit. God-fearing Jabez prayed, and God blessed him, enlarged his territory, and kept him from evil. Shepherd-king David prayed, and God created a clean heart and renewed a right spirit within him. Apocalyptic prophet Daniel prayed, and God dispatched the angel Gabriel with the answer. Reformer Hezekiah prayed, and God gave him fifteen extra years to live and to serve. Reluctant prophet Jonah prayed and was delivered from the belly of a big fish. Politician Nehemiah prayed, and a pagan king commissioned him to go home and rebuild the wall around Jerusalem.

In the New Testament Jesus prayed, and a basket of barley buns plus a few fish were multiplied into a meal that fed five thousand fellows and their families a bunch of lunch to munch for brunch. He prayed another time, and his dear friend Lazarus rose from the dead. Ten lepers prayed and were healed on the spot. The thief on the cross prayed and was saved right then and there. The disciples prayed, and the Spirit came, thousands were saved, signs and wonders occurred, and "the Good News about the wonderful grace of God"[5] was unleashed on the world. They prayed again, and an angel delivered Peter from prison. Then Peter prayed, and charitable Dorcas rose from the dead. The Apostle Paul and his side-kick Silas prayed, and a jailer and his family were saved from sin, then the two of them were saved from jail.

Moving forward from New Testament times, prayer has been the driving force, and often the saving force, of the church. In more than 20 centuries, without exception, every major spiritual awakening or revival that has occurred anywhere in the world began with the intercessory investment of believers on their knees. This makes sense. After all, the Church was born in a prayer meeting.

---

[5] Acts 20:24.

Prayer Partners with God

In prayer God partners with us to accomplish his work in our lives and his will in our world. The leader of the great eighteenth century revival that not only swept England but, according to some historians, saved that country from complete societal collapse, John Wesley, declared, "God does nothing except in response to believing prayer." What a thought: *God limits himself to our intercession.* So out of his great grace God invites us to unabashedly approach his throne to receive his mercy, find his grace, and lay hold of his help.

Speaking of seeking God's mercy and help, one of my daughters, during her junior and senior high years, had this sign in her room: "As long as there are exams, there WILL be prayer in school!"

Prayer is the greatest resource we have for experiencing the Christian life as it was meant to be lived. After all, remember, we are only as strong as our prayer life. Prayer is our highest privilege, our greatest tool, our strongest weapon, our surest defense, our dearest opportunity. It is the lifeblood of daily living and the lifeline to God's throne. Prayer is the "Adventureland" of the Christian life and the key to Christ's riches in glory. It is the birthright of the believer and the birthplace of God's miracles.

Mark and Betty Alton (the names aren't real, though the story is) were members of a church I served as pastor. They were going through a tough time when I came to their names on my list during my prayer time one morning. Mark had recently lost his job, Betty was too ill to work, and they had three young sons to provide for. As I prayed for them that morning, I felt prompted to buy a week's worth of groceries and deliver them to their home.

After acquiring the groceries, I drove to their house, knocked on the door, and when Betty answered I announced, "I have a grocery delivery for the Alton family." Then, making several trips to my car and back, I placed the sacks of food, one at a time, in the center of their kitchen floor.

After setting down the last sack, I looked up to see Mark, Betty, and their sons staring with tear-filled eyes at the groceries. Betty spoke. "Pastor, how did you know?"

"Know? Know what?" I asked.

"How did you know that not more than a couple hours ago we sat together around the kitchen table, held hands, and Mark prayed, 'Oh, Lord, if this family is going to eat this week, you're going to have to send someone with the groceries.'"

I didn't know, of course, but God did. Mark had presented their need to the Lord, and the Lord had dispatched me on an errand to provide for that need.

Grace assures us, as scripture promises us and experience tells us, of many things in this regard: That whatever we ask in Jesus's name, according to Jesus's will, in faith believing, the Father will do. That God hears and answers prayer, sometimes in great and mighty ways. That whatever our need—forgiveness, protection, wisdom, guidance, peace, strength, courage, comfort, healing, help, hope, or something else—we can and should pray about it.

Growing up, I loved sports. I still do. When I consider all the athletic analogies in Paul's New Testament letters, I figure I'm in good company. One of the sports I participated in during high school was wrestling, though I wasn't much good at it. Most of the time, I lost not by points but by getting pinned. For a while, I even held our high school's record for getting pinned the quickest: 19 seconds into the first round! Pretty pathetic. Believe it or not, eventually there was someone even worse than me who shaved several seconds off my record. But life is like that sometimes. You find yourself pinned on the mat of life by an opponent that just flat-out overwhelms you. And the name on the jersey your foe is wearing is "Cancer," or it's "Heartbreak," or "Rejection," or "Betrayal," or "Failure," or "Sorrow," or "Pain," or one of their other terrible teammates. It is then the believer is afforded the wonderful and sacred privilege of approaching the throne of a gracious God to seek his mercy, help, and grace.

Deathless Prayers

A prayer lifted to God today takes on a life of its own. Somewhere I came upon this quote, attributed to E. M. Bounds:

> Prayers are deathless. The lips that uttered them may be closed in death, the heart that felt them may have ceased to beat, but the prayers live before God, and God's heart is set on them and prayers outlive the lives of those who uttered them; they outlive a generation, outlive an age, outlive a world.

Professor, apologist, and author Peter Kreeft says the same thing in different words when he writes:

> I strongly suspect that if we saw all the difference even the tiniest of our prayers make, and all the people those little prayers were destined to affect, and all the consequences of those prayers down through the centuries, we would be so paralyzed with awe at the power of prayer that we would be unable to get up off our knees for the rest of our lives.

Now, that's saying something, but it shouldn't surprise us. Why wouldn't it be true?

David Livingstone valued prayer. I heard a speaker tell of when the great doctor, missionary, and explorer died, they found him in the morning by his bed on his knees. Late the night before, the natives who not only accompanied him everywhere but were his loyal friends, peeked into the little hut in which the doctor lived and saw him on his knees. When morning broke, he was still on his knees. Accustomed to seeing him in long sessions of prayer, they thought nothing of his still being there. Upon closer examination, though, they realized that sometime during the night his soul had gone on to God in glory. The preacher telling the story concluded by saying, "What a wonderful way to die—on your knees." I agree. Better yet, "What a wonderful way to *live*—on your knees.

One of the weekly tips in the running journal I use said, "Baby your knees. They're the largest joints in your body—and the most complex—a meeting place for thighbone, shinbone, and kneecap, all held together by strong ropes of ligaments."[6] Over my years as a runner I have learned, often the hard way, the truth of those words. But it's true not just physically. The knees are mighty important spiritually. Whether we're on our knees literally or figuratively, time spent in prayer is what holds everything in our lives together. After all, you're only as strong as your prayer life.

Years ago, a member of my church approached me saying, "Pastor, you emphasize prayer so much I'm afraid you're making prayer a substitute for action." I responded, not knowing if it was original or if I'd heard it somewhere, "Prayer is not a substitute for action. It is an action for which there is no substitute."

Prayer is not the lowest form of passivity, but the highest form of activity. It is humanity reaching up to divinity. It is our infirmity leaning on God's infinity. In prayer we come with empty hands but hopeful hearts. "Prayer is," as famed English preacher Charles Spurgeon noted in his classic comment, "the slender nerve that moves the muscle of omnipotence." Faith may be the wiring to God's miracles, but prayer flips the switch.

---

[6] Marty Jerome, "July 18," in *The Complete Runner's Day-By-Day Log 2020 Calendar* (Kansas City, MO: Andrews McMeel Publishing, 2019).

Next to knowing the Lord Jesus Christ as one's savior, shepherd, master, and faithful friend, the greatest privilege of the Christian life is conversation with God—that and the assurance that God hears and answers prayer.

A Long Drive and a Short Prayer

Eight-year-old Travis MacGuinness lay dying in the intensive care unit of C.S. Mott Children's Hospital, the pediatric wing of the University of Michigan Health System in Ann Arbor, Michigan. Daily I had been driving the eighty miles round trip to visit him and his parents, Mike and Connie, keeping vigil at his bedside. One day, rushing off in response to a church family's emergency at another hospital, I asked my youth pastor if he'd cover the Ann Arbor run to visit and pray with Travis and his parents.

Pastor Steve hit the road, had a brief visit with Mike and Connie at Travis's bedside, then prayed, "O Lord, please do something for young Travis that will amaze even the doctors." That was it! That's all he prayed. And without so much as an "in Jesus's name, amen," at the end.

I sent my bright, young, college-educated, seminary-trained, salaried and mileage-reimbursed associate eighty miles there and back to comfort a hurting family, and all he managed to eke out was a fourteen word one-sentence prayer.

An hour after Pastor Steve left the hospital, one of Travis's doctors rushed into the room. Having been summoned by a nurse and told Travis had dramatically revived, the doctor picked up the chart hanging on the foot of the bed, studied it, and then examined the eight-year-old. Turning to Mike and Connie he declared, "Well, I am *amazed*." Pastor Steve's brief but bold prayer had been answered. Just as he had asked, God had done something to "amaze even the doctors."

It is said God isn't interested so much in the *length* of our prayers as in the *depth* of them. What Pastor Steve's prayer lacked in length, it more than made up for in depth. It was bold, something Hebrews 4:16 not only commends but commands when it invites us to "come boldly to the throne of our gracious God. There we will receive his mercy, and we will find grace to help us when we need it most."

> Prayer is not overcoming God's
> reluctance, rather it is laying hold
> of his highest willingness.
> —Robert Savage

CHAPTER TWO

The Son of God Inspiring Us

Since we have a great High Priest who has entered heaven,
Jesus the Son of God, let us hold firmly to what we believe.
This High Priest of ours understands our weaknesses, for
he faced all of the same testings we do, yet he did not sin.

HEBREWS 4:14–15

When you pray, do you think about having Jesus in heaven, your High Priest, with ready access to the Father, interceding on your behalf, and, because of his experiences while on earth, he's in touch with what you go through? That's what Hebrews 4:14–15 is telling us. He's been through the wringer. He experienced testing and trouble, weakness and weariness, heartache and hurt, sadness and sorrow, all that we deal with, everything but the sinning. Now in heaven he lives and longs to meet our needs with God's grace and mercy. That alone, along with the realization it was his death on the cross that makes it possible for us to approach the throne of grace, ought to motivate and inspire our praying. But he inspires our praying in so many other ways as well. For one, by his prioritizing and practice of prayer while he was on earth, he is our mentor and model.

Our Lord's Example

The gospels make it clear that conversation with his Father was at the very core of Jesus's life on earth. He rose before daybreak to pray, climbed a mountain to pray, taught his disciples to pray, and purged the temple so people could pray. Prayers were his prelude to miracles. After breaking bread and serving wine at that last supper with his disciples, he poured out his heart in prayer for them and anyone who would ever follow him. He was at prayer when they came to arrest him. He prayed on the cross, where three of his last seven statements were prayers to his Father and a fourth statement was his answering the prayer of a criminal being crucified beside him.

There are few more beautiful illustrations of the priority of prayer in the life of Christ, along with his role as intercessor, than the time the disciples were caught in a storm on the Sea of Galilee while Jesus was on a mountain overlooking their battered boat on the tempestuous waters. He had gone there to pray. The event occurred between two of Jesus's miracles, the multiplication of the loaves and fish and his healing several people, leading Pastor David Redding to observe:

> That is what Jesus did between miracles—He visited their birthplace. Somehow the One who buttons His vest with stars, who wears earth as a ring around His little finger, lovingly gave His Son a lion's share of His authority; and Jesus emerged from those interviews bowed under a weight of glory and borne along on shining wings of peace.[7]

---

[7] David A. Redding, *The Miracles of Christ* (Westwood, NJ: Fleming H. Revell Company, 1964), 24–25.

This story of the disciples caught in one of Galilee's suddenly severe storms is recorded in three of the four gospels.[8] Rain-laden, charcoal clouds erupted in chilling, aerial explosions of saw-toothed lightning and reverberating thunder. Whistling, the wind whipped down the slopes surrounding the lake, attacking the boat like a voracious predator diving at its prey. Mountains in motion, the heaving waters flipped the helpless craft around like a plaything. The vessel tacked, tossed, and turned, mast groaning, sails tearing, timbers creaking, terrified disciples shouting orders at one another to do *this* and hold on to *that*.

The New Testament accounts don't specifically tell us Jesus was praying for them. They don't have to. He had gone there to pray in the first place. Besides, it is impossible to conceive of Christ, perched atop his pinnacle of prayer watching over them, *not* praying for them, his heart going out to them and his prayers going up for them. Today too, he watches over us, at the right hand of the Father, interceding for us,[9] passing on our prayers and adding some of his own, our heavenly high priest.

That night Jesus came to them stepping on the surging sea, settling down the unsettled waters and becoming his own answer to his own prayers, just as he comes to us today, the answer to our prayers in life's storms.

As our daughters, Theresa and Christy, were growing up, Noni and I tried to impart to them an understanding of a Christ who so identifies with our lot in life that he stands ready to receive our requests and respond according to his will and out of his power. From the eighteen years each spent under our roof, there is one of many experiences in prayer that stands head and shoulders above the rest. At the very least it was the most memorable, and for reasons you'll see.

The girls were in grade school and I had been invited to lead

---

[8] Matthew 14:22–33; Mark 6:46–52; and John 6:14–21.
[9] Romans 8:34.

in planting a new church. After much prayer and discussion, we said yes and immediately began house hunting in the community to which we'd be moving. Finally, Noni and I felt God had guided us to the house he had chosen for us. A bargain was struck with the owners and a closing date set.

Throughout the house hunt, we had been doing all we could to pull together funds for a down payment. Since we had always lived in church-owned homes, we had neither our own home nor the equity that would have come with that. We had some money in savings, managed to pull together a little more here and there, and sold a few things. Finally, we borrowed a large sum from my parents.[10] With the closing just two weeks off, I was confident we had exactly what we needed to bring to the table, until one day when I double-checked my figures. It was then I discovered that, thanks to my chronic mathematical ineptitude, I had miscalculated and we needed one thousand dollars more than we had.

That evening at supper, I said to the family, "I have some good news and some bad news. First, the bad news. I made a mistake. We are a thousand dollars short of what we need for the down payment on the house. Since we have already laid our hands on all the money we can, I have no idea where another thousand can possibly come from. Now, the good news. We can bring it to the Lord in prayer."

Following the meal, Noni and I held hands with Theresa and Christy around the table. "Lord," I began, "we said yes to this church plant because you led us to. And we believe you led us to the house we found. Now we find ourselves shy of what we need by one thousand dollars. Please provide the money we need or show us whatever else you have in mind."

A few days later my oldest daughter, Theresa, eight years old at the time, and I were having our weekly breakfast date at the local

---

[10] Yes, we paid them back.

McDonald's restaurant. Macs was having a contest called "You Deserve a Break Today"™ and we had been faithfully checking out the prize stamps in the little envelopes that came with our meal each week. We had scored some free French fries and a couple complimentary soft drinks throughout the contest, but that was it, and this was the last day. After sitting down at our table and saying grace, we began to open the prize envelopes we'd been given. Coming to the last one, I found myself staring at a stamp that read, "Instant Winner—$1,000."

"Oh, Dad, you've made a mistake," Theresa replied when I told her. "Let me see that," she demanded. Then, she remembered before I did. "Dad, we prayed for a thousand dollars!"

The next week a reporter from the local newspaper interviewed us. We told him the whole story: The church plant, the house hunt, the down payment shortage, the prayer, the answer. When the story was published in the paper a few days later, fully the top half of page three, the headline over the account and a large picture of Theresa and me read, "Pastor Prays for and Gets a Break."

The lead sentence to the article stated, "God and Ronald McDonald teamed up to give the Rev. Thomas Ramundo a break the other day." A detailed account of our story followed. Then the reporter finished with a flourish, stating McDonald's should change their slogan to "You Deserve a Miracle Today." And our family agrees. In fact, it's what we call a real "McMiracle."

Twenty-five years later on the anniversary of our thousand-dollar miracle, Theresa, now with a family of her own, met me for breakfast at a McDonald's. We ordered Egg McMuffins and hash browns, plus coffee for me and orange juice for her, just what we'd ordered that day long ago. We sat down, said grace, joyfully reminisced over the newspaper article, and finished by thanking the Lord for his faithfulness then and always, for that memory has often inspired us to trust more and pray on.

Praying the Prayer of Prayers

Another way the Lord Jesus inspires our praying is through the prayer he gave us, commonly called "The Lord's Prayer." Through it we offer God worship and praise, seek his kingdom, will, and forgiveness, and trust him for his provision and protection. It is not, however, my intention here to plumb the depths of this prayer of prayers. Far too many saints and scholars have already done that for me to think I'd have anything new or better to offer. However, I want to suggest some simple reasons why the Lord's Prayer can be a regular and worthwhile part of our personal and corporate prayer lives.

First, *it is the prayer that never fails.* It comes straight from the Lord Jesus Christ himself, who taught it in response to his disciples' request that he teach them to pray,[11] and as such it can't help but be spot on. Some people see it as an outline for praying. I have sometimes used it that way in both personal and public prayer. But most of the time I prefer to use it, as most people do, word for word as Jesus taught it, though we may differ on the "debts" versus "trespasses" part. I'm a "debts and debtors" man myself, and I am going to tell you why.

There are a handful of different words in the New Testament for sin. The one used in the Lord's Prayer, *opheilema*, refers to "a balance owed," a debt. Every time we sin, we go into debt to God, and it is a debt we cannot possibly pay. Only our honest confession and sincere repentance, followed by God's grace-driven forgiveness, can balance the books. That's why I'm for using "debts" in the Lord's prayer, though one time, following my explanation for that, my grandson, Baily, opined, "Grandpa, why don't we just say 'sins' if that's what it's talking about?" Still, when seeking forgiveness or praying anything else in the Lord's Prayer, it is the prayer that never fails.

---

[11] Luke 11:1–4.

Another reason I'm sold on regular use of the Lord's Prayer is that *it perfectly reflects the will of God*. It must, after all—look who the author is. Think of how often you pray about something, not being quite sure you're in synch with the will of the Father. There is no doubt you're praying God's will when you're praying the prayer he gave us, be it in general or over a particular need.

The third reason I highly appreciate the prayer Jesus taught us is that *it covers all the bases*. It contains all possible petitions. Can you conceive of any area of existence and experience not covered by it? It is not possible to sincerely pray the Lord's Prayer without covering every need for loved ones and others, as well as ourselves, the kingdom, and the world. It even reaches into eternity. When we pray the Lord's Prayer we are covering, in six statements, *everything!*

On August 23, 1969, "the Mrs. and me" matrimonially merged our lives from that day forward, promising and meaning it, to love and to cherish each other, come what may, for the rest of our lives. The vows we exchanged didn't leave any wiggle room or loopholes, as anyone who takes them seriously knows. They cover every possibility—good and bad, poverty and plenty, sickness and health, and are unfailingly 100 percent prophetic.

As we knelt at the altar on our wedding day, our soloist sang a well-known rendition of "The Lord's Prayer." We had no idea then, but it was a preview of things to come. For over the years, as we have had our share of the bad-poverty-sickness part of the vows, the Lord's Prayer has come in handy, especially a few times when the challenges were so daunting we despaired to even know how to pray. The answer just didn't come, at least not the way we thought it should and would, and after a while we ran out of ways to even pray about it. At that point, rather than cease praying about it altogether, we started praying the Lord's Prayer over it, knowing we were praying God's perfect will in every possible way about the matter. That brought not only comfort, but eventually resolution, though there were a couple times it took years.

Some years ago, Noni and I decided to start offering the Lord's Prayer on an almost daily basis, usually at the end of our Bible and prayer time, though sometimes as a mealtime grace. In addition to the reasons already given, we made that decision in part because the prayer wasn't being used in church as much as it used to be, and we missed it the way you miss a dear, old friend.

We also decided to pray it daily because we knew a grandchild or two would be with us from time to time, and we wanted them to learn it. So, sister and brother Natalie and Baily learned the prayer at our table. I can still remember the morning their younger cousin, Brooke, all of four years old at the time and for whom we were providing regular childcare, sputtered out words and phrases of it here and there as Grandma and I prayed it, and then she put an exclamation point at the end, effervescing with a shout: "For thine is the KINGDOM, and the POWER, and the GLORY, FOREVER, AAAAA-MEN!"

Finally, we took up the Lord's Prayer as a daily discipline because we knew that with the relentless onward march of time there could come a day for one or both of us when our mental faculties would be failing. Just maybe, we reasoned, having constantly used the prayer over the years would leave it imprinted so deeply on our brains and in our hearts that even in the face of dementia we could still say it—not only say it, but somewhere in the ever-darkening recesses of our mind, still be touched by its rich meaning.

You may wonder about that last paragraph, but throughout my years visiting and conducting services in nursing homes, I have seen senior saints who were otherwise unresponsive suddenly come to life and participate aloud when an old hymn, a familiar scripture like the Twenty-Third Psalm or the Lord's Prayer was used. Although normally incapable of communication, here they were, singing or saying the words!

There are many reasons for us to pray the praises, petitions, and provisions of the prayer Jesus taught his disciples—just one of the ways the Son of God inspires our prayer lives. But there is yet another way the Son of God provides inspiration for our praying.

The Gardener God

Mary Magdalene was right the first time, you know, that Easter morning not far from the empty tomb. He *was* the gardener. Mistaking the risen Christ for the garden keeper, she addressed him as such.[12] But the instant he spoke her name in response, she knew it was Jesus. Still, he was a gardener, "*the* Gardener," who had come to pull the weeds of grief and hurt from the soil of her sorrowing soul, plant the seeds of resurrection power and great joy in her broken heart, water them with the wonders of his grace, and grow in her a garden of faith, hope, love, and life. To say it with songwriter Austin Miles's old Easter song in mind, it all begins as Jesus walks with her and talks with her and assures her she is his own.[13]

---

[12] John 20:14–15.

[13] C. Austin Miles (1868–1946) wrote this gospel song, "In the Garden," also known by the title, "I Come to the Garden Alone," in 1912. Miles was a pharmacist turned writer, editor, and publisher. According to his great-granddaughter, the song was written in a dark, damp, dreary, and cold basement in Pitman, New Jersey, "that didn't even have a window in it let alone a view of a garden." It became an instant hit when evangelist Billy Sunday used it in his gospel campaigns. Over the years it has been recorded by such greats of the music world as Roy Rogers and Dale Evans, Tennessee Ernie Ford, Perry Como, Rosemary Clooney, Doris Day, Elvis Presley, Willie Nelson, Glen Campbell, Brad Paisley, and Johnny Cash. Sometimes criticized for what some consider its overly sentimental take on Mary Magdalene's Easter morning encounter with the risen Lord Jesus, the chorus in particular resonates with many who value times of intimate communion and conversation with the Lord: "And He walks with me, and He talks with me, and He tells me I am His own; and the joy we share as we tarry there, none other has ever known."

If prayer is anything, it is walking and talking with the Gardener God, enjoying communion and conversation that yields a rich harvest of worship and wonder, surrender and strength, resources and miracles. And along with that there comes a crop of such fruit of the Spirit as "love, joy, peace, patience, kindness, goodness, faithfulness, gentleness, and self-control."[14]

We should pray when we are in a
praying mood, for it would be sinful
to neglect so fair an opportunity.
We should pray when we are not in a
proper mood, for it would be dangerous
to remain in so unhealthy a condition.
—Charles Spurgeon

---

[14] Galatians 5:22–23.

The Word of God Instructing Us

For the word of God is alive and powerful. It is sharper than the sharpest two-edged sword, cutting between soul and spirit, between joint and marrow. It exposes our innermost thoughts and desires. Nothing in all creation is hidden from God. Everything is naked and exposed before his eyes, and he is the one to whom we are accountable.

HEBREWS 4:12–13

It is significant that the teaching on prayer we've been looking at in Hebrews 4:14–16 is preceded by these two verses about the Word of God. D. L. Moody said, "I believe we should know better how to pray if we knew our Bibles better." In other words, we pray best when we are in touch with God's Word first. In this chapter, then, we are going to look at how God's Word both instructs and informs our praying. That is, how it teaches us all we need to know about *how* to pray, as well as a great deal of what we ought to be praying about *when* we pray.

In his contemporary rendering of the Bible, *The Message*, Eugene Peterson, known as "the pastor's pastor," serves up these two verses this way:

God means what he says. What he says goes. His powerful Word is sharp as a surgeon's scalpel, cutting through everything, whether doubt or defense, laying us open to listen and obey. Nothing and no one is impervious to God's Word. We can't get away from it—no matter what.[15]

These verses are clear: The Word of God brings us face to face with ourselves, causing us to see ourselves as God sees us. It cuts into our innermost thoughts, deepest desires, and the motivations that move us, exposing us for what we really are. It is no wonder, then, that New Testament writer James said looking into the Bible is like peering into a mirror—it gives us a good look at what we need to change.[16] As such, it reveals the things in our life we need to deal with in prayer.

Along with that, when God's Word has permeated our minds and penetrated our hearts, it will overflow into our praying, flooding our prayers with God's wisdom and will.

The Believer's Primer on Prayer

As we saw in the first chapter, the Bible is in many ways a book about prayer and a book of prayer, filled with teaching on prayer along with examples of people praying and God answering. While many good books have been written *about* prayer, the Bible is the best textbook *on* prayer. It is the believer's primer on prayer.

Some years ago, I led a congregation in an exercise we called, "Forty Days with Great Prayers of the Bible." The idea certainly wasn't original with me, but hitchhiking on the significance of the number forty in scripture, we spent each of that many days on a

---

[15] *The Message: The Bible in Contemporary Language,* copyright 1993, 1994, 1995, 1996, 2000, 2001, 2002. Used by permission of NavPress Publishing Group, Colorado Springs, CO.
[16] James 1:22–25.

different Bible passage about prayer. On Sundays, I preached on one of the seven passages those participating had read that week. We started with Abraham's prayer for Sodom and ended with the prayers of heavenly worship in Revelation.

In between, we encountered Moses's prayers for Israel and Nehemiah's prayer for Jerusalem, Joshua's prayer in defeat and Jehoshaphat's prayer for victory, David's prayers in Psalms and Daniel's prayers in Babylon. We pondered Hannah's prayer for a child and Solomon's prayer for wisdom, Hezekiah's prayer for healing and Isaiah's prayer for mercy.

We learned from the Lord's Prayer in Matthew 6, Jesus's prayer for his followers in John 17, the disciples' Pentecost-producing prayers in Acts 1 and 2, the early church's prayer for boldness in Acts 4, and Paul's prayer for the church in Ephesians 3.

All those and more we read about and I preached on, and before we were through, the temperature of our church's prayer life had risen several degrees. Renewal was spreading like a wildfire through our ranks. Our church was growing faster than ever as we led more and more people to faith in Christ. And all because we had taken a deep dive into what the Bible has to teach, illustrate, and encourage about prayer, and then put what we were learning to work in our lives and church.

Since the Bible has so much to teach us about prayer, we're going to invest the rest of this chapter in examining several biblical principles that govern and guide how we pray.

Instructions and Injunctions from Scripture[17]

A quick survey reveals scripture teaches us to pray with sincerity, honesty, and intensity, as well as to pray humbly, thoughtfully,

---

[17] If you are interested in further study of basic biblical guidelines on how to pray, I recommend *The Forgotten Rules of Prayer* by K. C. Hairston, (Memphis, TN: Hairston, 2016), a survey of twenty-eight rules of prayer found in scripture.

expectantly, respectfully, patiently, specifically, submissively, and selflessly.

Scripture also teaches us to pray according to God's will and in faith believing, and that some prayers require fasting along with them.

As with all the believer thinks or does, the Bible shows us prayer should be for the glory of God and in Jesus's name. And when we pray in his name, it isn't so much saying the phrase as though it's a magical incantation, as it is the attitude of our heart in reverence and recognition of who God is, what he does, and all he means to us.

One of the Bible's biggest (and toughest) injunctions on prayer is found in the Lord's Prayer, where it tells us that prayers for God to forgive our offenses against him must be preceded by a spirit of forgiveness on our part toward those who have offended us. Sometimes I can't help but flinch when I think about that, but I have grown to take it more seriously than I once did.

Paul instructs us to wrap our petitions in thanksgiving.[18] Praise is the wind in the sails of our prayers. It propels them on their way. The Lord's Prayer begins and ends with worship and praise. When we begin our prayer times that way, we not only rightfully honor God, we set the tone for presenting the petitions and requests that will follow.

To keep me from plunging willy-nilly into my lists of prayer concerns and requests every time I pray, on the first page of my prayer journals I write in large lettering, "ALWAYS BEGIN WITH WORSHIP, PRAISE, AND THANKSGIVING." That serves to remind me to commence my prayer times worshipping God for who he is (holy, just, unchanging, faithful, merciful, loving, forgiving, all-powerful, all-knowing, ever-present, and more). It also leads me to thank him for all of his blessings and answers to prayer.

---

[18] Philippians 4:6.

To keep me in a fresh supply of praises for my prayer times, I make daily deposits in my "Bank of Blessings." Back in pre-computerized times we had a little book in which we recorded our savings deposits, withdrawals, and balance. We called it a "bank book." Now I have a "thank book," where I daily record my blessings and answers to prayer, my deposits in my Bank of Blessings.

Moving on to another biblical principle of prayer: In Matthew 18:19–20 Jesus teaches us there's additional power when we pray in agreement with other believers. "If two of you agree here on earth concerning anything you ask, my Father in heaven will do it for you. For where two or three are gathered together as my followers, I am there among them."

Psalm 66:18–19 makes it clear that we must pray with a clean heart and a clear conscience: "If I had not confessed the sin in my heart, the Lord would not have listened. But God did listen! He paid attention to my prayer." 1 Peter 3:7 ups the ante for husbands when it tells them to treat their wives with understanding and honor as coheirs of God's grace *so their prayers won't go unanswered.* And Proverbs 28:9 should make us all sit up and pay attention when it tells us "God detests the prayers of a person who ignores the [his] law."

Another thing scripture makes clear is that God isn't keen on empty promises made when we pray. Personally, I prefer to shy away from making vows when I pray. It seems a little too much like I'm trying to pay God to come through for me. "If you do that for me, Lord, I'll do this for you." But if you're going to make a vow, keep Ecclesiastes 5:4–5 in mind: "When you make a promise to God, don't delay in following through, for God takes no pleasure in fools. Keep all the promises you make to him. It is better to say nothing than to make a promise and not keep it."

The Prayer That Prevails Is
the Prayer That Travails

―――

The Bible also teaches us that prayers that prevail are offered with passion and persistence. Folks used to call that kind of praying "travailing prayer." Consider Blind Bartimaeus in Mark 10, crying out, "Jesus, Son of David, have mercy on me!"[19] And when the annoyed crowd told him to knock it off, he bellowed even louder, "Son of David, have mercy on me!" Now, that's passionate persistence. It got Jesus's attention, and the Great Physician healed him of his blindness. The sight-seeking Bartimaeus prevailed because he travailed.

Right after he taught the disciples the Lord's Prayer, Jesus shared the story of the insistent individual who, in the middle of the night, kept knocking on his neighbor's door until the neighbor finally got up and gave him the food he needed. Jesus says the neighbor finally responded because of the door-banger's bold insistence. The point of the parable is not that God is reluctant to answer our prayers, rather the power of passion and perseverance in petitioning him.

In his sermon titled "Jacob Wrestling," John Wesley said, "Those who would have the blessing of Christ must be in good earnest, and be importunate for it." *Importunate,* an adjective not common in speech today, can best be defined by some of its synonyms: insistent, persistent, tenacious, dogged, unrelenting, tireless, and aggressive. Strong terms. But then again, strong prayers are all those things. And strong prayers help us become prayer strong.

Often, a part of praying with passionate persistence is asking with "shameless audacity," an expression I first heard from a friend, Ron Burley. Ron shared this with me, and with his permission I share it with you:

―――

[19] v. 46–52.

We raised eight children, four older and four younger with a good spread in between. When our fifth was born it was like he was the boy with six parents. Leighton was one little boy who had no shame when it came to asking me for things. Outright over-the-top requests. The older four would be taken back with his bold requests sometimes. One night at the table he asked me for something with shameless audacity. The older four were taken back in shock that this young kid could be so bold and tenacious. One of them reprimanded him: "Leighton, have you no shame?" Leighton, in his eight-year-old innocence relied, "Why can't I ask? He's my dad." Maybe that's how we should be praying.

Knowing he's our Father should give us the confidence to be irrepressible intercessors praying with faith and fervor.

To be blunt, I'd have to say that sometimes our prayers don't have enough oomph to get past the ceiling, let alone reach the gates of heaven and touch the heart of God. Here's where Maltie Babcock offers a word of caution: "Our prayers must mean *something* to us if they are to mean *anything* to God." Prayers put on mindless cruise control just go through the motions, lacking intensity, passion, and shameless audacity. Prayers like that are nullified by our underwhelming passion and suppressed perspiration.

Now I don't mean to suggest that the measure of prayers that prevail is raising a raucous ruckus. You can have passion of purpose and depth of desire without being loud and crazy. We don't have to carry on as though God is deaf. One of scripture's most passionate petitioners, Hannah, was so intent and intense in her praying she gave Eli the priest the mistaken impression she was drunk even though she wasn't making a sound, only moving her lips.[20] Still, we want million-dollar answers to ten-cent prayers. Harold Lindsell, author of *When You Pray*, writes, "Prayer that is effective springs from an irresistible and unquenchable intensity which will be rewarded."[21]

Turn the Bible into Prayer

Along with teaching us principles of prayer, scripture provides some of the raw material, the very phrases, praises, and petitions we might offer when we pray. Pastor, preacher, and poet Robert Murray McCheyne, who, in just under twenty-nine years of life (1813-1843) and eight years of ministry was used of God to revitalize the Church of Scotland, advised "Turn the Bible into prayer."

The book of Psalms is the obvious first place to turn when talking about praying the Bible. So many prayers in Psalms flow in first-person communication to God from a heart of joy, peace, excitement, praise, pain, anger, anxiety, disillusionment, or any number of emotions we deal with.

Whatever you think of using printed prayers, the psalms are in a class by themselves. How could the following collection of verses blended together to form a prayer of praise ever feel like a "canned prayer"? Go ahead, pause a moment, take a deep breath, and pray with praise:

> O Lord, our Lord, your majestic name fills the earth! Your glory is higher than the heavens. (Psalm 8:1)

> I will praise you, Lord, with all my heart; I will tell of all the marvelous things you have done. I will

---

[20] 1 Samuel 1:12–13.

[21] Harold Lindsell, *When You Pray* (Wheaton, IL: Tyndale House Publishers, 1969), 64.

be filled with joy because of you. I will sing praises to your name, O Most High. (Psalm 9:1)

You will show me the way of life, granting me the joy of your presence and the pleasures of living with you forever. (Psalm 16:11)

I love you, Lord; you are my strength. (Psalm 18:1)

My heart is confident in you, O God; my heart is confident. No wonder I can sing your praises! (Psalm 57:7)

I have seen you in your sanctuary and gazed upon your power and glory. Your unfailing love is better than life itself; how I praise you! I will praise you as long as I live, lifting up my hands to you in prayer. You satisfy me more than the richest feast. I will praise you with songs of joy. (Psalm 63:2–5)

Not just praise, the psalms supply words for our greatest struggles, deepest hurts, and moments of sheer desperation. Here's an example of a prayer to be prayed when life is beating up on you:

O Lord, I have come to you for protection; don't let me be disgraced. Save me, for you do what is right. Turn your ear to listen to me; rescue me quickly. Be my rock of protection, a fortress where I will be safe. (Psalm 31:1–2)

Have mercy on me, O God, have mercy! I look to you for protection. I will hide beneath the shadow of your wings until the danger passes by ... My heart is confident in you, O God; my heart is confident. (Psalm 57:1, 7)

Lord, hear my prayer! Listen to my plea! Don't turn away from me in my time of distress. Bend down to listen, and answer me quickly when I call to you. (Psalm 102:1–2)

More than once, awash in guilt and shame for some wrongful thought, word, act, or habit, I have appropriated David's prayer of confession for restoration after the prophet Nathan had bluntly confronted him for taking Uriah's wife and life:

Have mercy on me, O God, because of your unfailing love. Because of your great compassion, blot out the stain of my sins. Wash me clean from my guilt. Purify me from my sin. For I recognize my rebellion; it haunts me day and night. Against you, and you alone, have I sinned ... Your judgment against me is just ... Purify my sins, and I will be clean; wash me, and I will be whiter than snow. Oh, give me back my joy again ... Don't keep looking at my sins. Remove the stain of my guilt. Create in me a clean heart, O God, renew a loyal spirit within me ... Don't take your Holy Spirit from me. Restore to me the joy of your salvation. (Psalm 51:1–12)

An excellent psalm to pray almost any time for any reason is Psalm 139. Its twenty-four verses major on the omniscient (all-knowing), omnipresent (all-present), omnipotent (all-powerful) characteristics of God in practical, comforting, inspiring ways. Go ahead, look it up. Ponder all it says and means. Keep it in mind as something you might pray from time to time.

Even if you don't use all of Psalm 139 as a prayer, the last two verses are in themselves an excellent way to invite God to evaluate you: "Search me, O God, and know my heart; test me and known my anxious thoughts. Point out anything in me that offends you, and lead me along the path of everlasting life." Pray that, then be still and open to what the Lord may bring into your mind and heart.

Of course, most scriptures don't readily lend themselves to first-person word-for-word use, but many provide excellent material to set the direction of a prayer. They help us focus our thoughts and frame our words. Take, for instance, Isaiah 40:28–31, the uplifting "soar on wings like eagles" passage. Drawing from its thoughts, you or I might pray: "Oh Lord, my everlasting God, Creator of all the earth; you never grow weak or weary. You neither flag nor fail. When I run out of steam you are able to recharge my batteries. Even those who are young and strong can get worn out and need help. Right now, I am shot, done in, all out of gas, and ready to go to pieces. Please give me new strength, so I can soar eagle-like on high, run without weariness, and march on without giving out."

Occasionally a story will pop up in the news about an individual who, after years of living in squalor, has died, only for someone to discover in their home a hidden treasure trove of cash. We are shocked that someone with great wealth available failed to use it. We, too, often ignore valuable treasure: The wording and material for prayer that could be mined from the Word of God. For too many of us, praying the Bible, be it word for word or by incorporating its thoughts and truths in prayer, is a sadly underutilized means of coming before the throne of grace.

Discerning God's Will

Another way scripture can inform our praying is when we are seeking to discern if a request we want to offer is in line with God's will. Let me suggest one simple method for your consideration.[22] It will not apply to all potential requests, but it will help with many. It is based on the fact we don't have to waste a lot of time foraging about, trying to figure out if a prayer request is right or not when the answer is already in God's Word. This approach involves the use of two questions, each question one side of the same coin.

First question: Is there anything in scripture—a command, a teaching, an example, a warning, a principle, or a promise—that prohibits or discourages this request?

One time a married man came for counseling. He told me he was considering having an affair. He asked me to pray with him that he might know if it was God's will or not. I told him we didn't need to pray because we already knew the answer. "Does the seventh commandment ring a bell?" I asked, and then I quoted Exodus 20:14 to him as it thunders in the King James Version: "Thou shalt not commit adultery." Case closed. Admittedly that's an extreme example, but when scripture clearly prohibits, warns against, or discourages something, there's no reason to waste your time or God's praying about it.

Second question: Is there anything in God's Word—a command, a teaching, an example, a promise, or a principle—that prescribes or encourages this request?

Trust me when I say that I am not the sharpest knife in the drawer. I am at best of average intelligence (and have the IQ to prove it!). If God made me this way, is it right for me to ask him to make me smarter, at least in some matters or situations?

Well, King Solomon, when handed a blank check by God and told to fill in whatever he wanted, prayed not for riches or fame but for wisdom and knowledge. God gave it to him.[23] So, there's an example.

---

[22] While I develop it a bit differently, the spark that ignited the approach I share here is in Tony Evans's book *The Victorious Christian Life* (Nashville, TN: Thomas Nelson, 1994), 138–39.

[23] 2 Chronicles 1:7–14.

Years later, that same king, older and even wiser, pulled together the book of Proverbs, every one of its thirty-one chapters extolling not only the value of wisdom but the virtue of attaining it. Thus, there's an entire book of the Bible full of teachings, principles, and assurances on the value of pursuing wisdom.

Then, in the New Testament, James tells us, "Now if any of you lacks wisdom, he should ask God—who gives to all generously and ungrudgingly—and it will be given to him."[24] Now, that's what I call a promise. And that, coupled with what we saw from Solomon and Proverbs, tells me that on the basis of God's Word, he welcomes my request for wisdom.

"But," you say, "those two questions won't help me figure out God's will for everything." True. And we'll talk about that further in chapter 5 when we examine how the Holy Spirit aids us in discovering God's will. But for now, suffice it to say that when you have given serious prayer and careful thought to a situation, and have perhaps sought godly guidance from a trusted fellow believer or two, you may be confident the Lord will direct your steps. And his direction includes the assurance that even if you do make a mistake, his grace is great enough to either get you back on the right track or use it for good.

The Great Omission

Another area of prayer for which we find clear biblical instruction is the directive to pray not only for all people, but for governmental leaders and heads of state as well. Writes Paul to young Pastor Timothy:

> I urge you, first of all, to pray for all people. Ask
> God to help them; intercede on their behalf, and

---

[24] Christian Standard Bible, copyright 2017 by Holman Bible Publishers. Used by permission.

> give thanks for them. Pray this way for kings
> and all who are in authority so that we can live
> peaceful and quiet lives marked by godliness
> and dignity. This is good and pleases God our
> Savior, who wants everyone to be saved and to
> understand the truth.[25]

Among many Christians and in many churches today, Paul's words here are so tragically ignored they amount to "The Great Omission." In a climate increasingly hostile to Christian beliefs and behavior, morals and values, and in a culture that seems to be disintegrating before our very eyes, I can't help but wonder how much better off our troubled world would be if God's people everywhere obeyed this biblical injunction.

Anyone old enough to remember can picture the sights and sounds of September 11, 2001—the day terrorists took down the twin towers of the World Trade Center in New York City, and with them, the lives of nearly three thousand Americans.

That awful Tuesday morning found our church staff huddled around a television in one of the classrooms, watching as the tragic events unfolded. Eventually, we had a prayer time together and then went our separate ways to get to work. I was in my office at the start of the noon hour when my secretary poked her head in the door. "Excuse me, Pastor, but I think you'll want to come down to the sanctuary and see what's happening."

Now, our church had become known throughout the community for its emphasis on prayer, and we even advertised that our doors were always open for those who would like a place to pray.[26] Regularly, both members of our church and others from the community would take us up on the opportunity, but I was unprepared for the sight before me. As I peered through

---

[25] 1 Timothy 2:1–4.

[26] If you're wondering about security, we had the staff, including facilities staff, to keep a watchful eye on people entering the building.

the lobby windows into the sanctuary, I could see the place was packed—front row to back, aisle to aisle. It would have taken the proverbial shoehorn to squeeze in one more person. A few were from my congregation; most I did not recognize. While many prayed quietly, others wept openly.

I called my wife, so choked up I could barely speak, and told her what was happening. She quickly drove to the church and together we walked down a side aisle to the front to join those who were kneeling along the altar in prayer.

What drew these people to our church, many from other churches, and some who only knew our church from driving past it or hearing about it? You know the answer to that. It was the collective hurt and fear an entire nation was feeling, and the need to turn to the God who is our only sufficient refuge and strength in times of trouble.[27] They had come to pray for our country, for our leaders, and for three thousand suddenly grieving families. Many were obeying Paul's instructions to Timothy, perhaps for the first time, without even realizing it. That same scene was repeated that night, the place packed again, only this time for an announced prayer service.

Paul's words to Timothy, along with God's promise to Israel that surely applies to us as well, is this: If God's people, who are called by his name, will humble themselves, pray, seek his face and repent, he will hear from heaven and forgive and heal their land.[28] *This* is an area of prayer we can no longer afford to ignore as much as we do.

Don't Just Stand There—Pray Something

As we have seen, scripture has much to teach us about prayer. Still, you can be an accomplished scholar of everything God's

---

[27] Psalm 46:1.

[28] 2 Chronicles 7:14.

Word teaches on prayer, and it will get you nowhere if you don't actually pray. Yes, pray. Just do it. Ask. Setting aside a regular time and place will help, but do it. Keeping a written record of petitions and praises—that is, requests and answers—may be helpful too, but go for it.

Jim Cymbala, author of the contemporary classic on prayer, *Fresh Wind, Fresh Fire*, writes: "If we call upon the Lord, he has promised in his Word to answer, to bring the unsaved to himself, to pour out his Spirit among us. If we don't call upon the Lord, he has promised nothing—nothing at all. It's as simple as that."[29]

Billy Graham said, "Heaven is full of answers to prayer for which no one bothered to ask." Yes, of course God knows our need, and he knows it better than we do. Still, he wants us to ask. God knew Hannah desperately wanted a son, but she had to ask for one. God knew David was sorry for his sins, but the king had to ask for forgiveness. The Lord knew perfectly well that the Sennacherib-led Assyrian army in all its might and muscle was ready to decimate Hezekiah and his kingdom. Still, Hezekiah had to ask for deliverance. Jesus knew Bartimaeus wanted to be able to see, yet he made him say the words.

The same holds true for us. There are many wonderful assurances given and promises made in the Bible for us to claim. Thousands of them. But just because something is promised by God in the Bible doesn't negate the need to pray for it.

But why does God want us to ask in the first place? That's something any thinking person can't help but wonder. If God is sovereign and knows what's best for us, why do we need to ask? Jesus even tells us, "Your Father knows exactly what you need even before you ask him!"[30] If that's the case, why doesn't he just go ahead and provide?

---

[29] Jim Cymbala, *Fresh Wind, Fresh Fire* (Grand Rapids, MI: Zondervan Publishing House, 1997), 27.

[30] Matthew 6:8.

I'm not sure the Bible gives us a straight-out answer to this question, but several reasons can be deduced. For one, the fact he wants us to ask ought to be reason enough to ask, shouldn't it? Still, we wonder why. Along with a reason mentioned earlier in this book, that God choses to partner with us in prayer to accomplish his will in the world and in our lives, there are other reasons he may want us to ask. For instance, prayer is an acknowledgment on our part that we are utterly dependent on God. Every time we come before the Lord with our requests, we are signing a declaration, not of independence but of dependence.

Another reason, one I've learned from personal experience, is that as I keep praying about a particular need, my focus on the need itself becomes clearer and what I should be asking God for is increasingly clarified and modified. Then too, asking prepares us to receive the answer. When the answer comes, having asked for it, we are in a position to recognize where it came from and we are more likely to thank and praise God than if he just dropped it in our lap without our first bringing it to him.

James, frank as can be, says we don't have what we need because we don't *ask* for it.[31] While so many wonder about the problem of *unanswered prayer* (we'll address that in the next chapter), more basic and troubling is the problem of *unoffered prayer*.

We don't sing it much in church anymore, but the old hymn, "What a Friend We Have in Jesus," lays it on the line in the last half of the first verse:

Oh, what peace we often forfeit,
Oh, what needless pain we bear,
All because we do not carry,
Everything to God in prayer.[32]

---

[31] James 4:2.
[32] Joseph Scriven, "What a Friend We Have in Jesus," 1855.

The lyrics lament forfeited peace and unnecessary pain because we don't avail ourselves of the privilege of prayer.

The choice is ours. We can be a *care worrier* or a *prayer warrior*. We can hold our problems inward or send them upward. As influential nineteenth century English preacher, Charles Spurgeon, bluntly put it, "God never shuts his storehouses until you shut your mouth."

The Word of God has a lot to teach us about prayer, the most basic being: Ask. Just ask.

> Heaven is full of answers to prayer
> for which no one bothered to ask.
> —Billy Graham

CHAPTER FOUR

The Riches of God
Encouraging Us

*And my God will supply all your needs according
to his riches in glory in Christ Jesus.*

———

To reinforce the point addressed at the end of the last chapter
and to set the tone for this chapter, we step into a kitchen in a
church I pastored for eighteen years. In that kitchen, the door
to each cabinet had the cabinet's contents labelled on it in raised
white vinyl lettering. The wording on one of the cabinets read:
"UNCLAIMED DISHES." These were, no doubt, dishes people
had used to bring in food for potluck dinners, then forgot and
left behind. Some kind soul had washed them and put them in
the "UNCLAIMED DISHES" cabinet until the rightful owner
might reclaim them. The strange thing, though, is that the
"UNCLAIMED DISHES" cabinet had a padlock on it! So, I
concluded this is where dishes went to die.

When I ponder the meaning of this curious cabinet, I imagine
myself ambling one day down the golden pavement of Heaven's

———

[33] Christian Standard Bible.

———

main street. Suddenly, the Lord joins me on my stroll and says, "Thomas, walk with me." He then leads me through the shining streets of the celestial city and out a back gate into the heavenly countryside. Side by side we hike up a steep hill. Reaching the crest of the hill, I look down into the valley before me and see the biggest, widest, longest, highest building I have ever seen.

With a wink and a motion to follow him, Jesus leads me down into the valley and up to this monstrous—let's call it warehouse. As we approach the door, the Lord produces a key and as he unlocks a padlock securing the door, I notice on the door, in raised white vinyl lettering, the words "UNCLAIMED ANSWERS."

Swinging the door open, he motions for me to enter first. I step inside and find myself staring at rows and rows of shelves reaching as high as a skyscraper and stretching as far as I can see to the left, to the right, and straight ahead. The shelves are jam packed with many things. Some I recognize as material objects. Others appear to be intangible blessings of various sorts, and yet I can identify them as such.

"Lord," I ask, "what is this? What are all these things?"

"Oh, my child," he responds, his voice heavy with sadness, "These are the unclaimed answers to prayers-never-uttered over the centuries. These are the things I was prepared to give to believers, but they never asked for them. They had a need and never presented it to me. All I wanted was for them to ask."

I survey the shelves again, and realize I am looking at God's (albeit unclaimed) riches in glory. All *he* asks is that *we* ask.

Needs or "Greeds"

So here we are, back where the last chapter ended, where we noted James said we don't have because we don't ask. But after James points that out, he immediately goes on to say, "And even when you ask, you don't get it because your motives are all wrong—you want only what will give you pleasure."[34] When Paul tells us the Lord will provide for us out of his riches in glory, notice he says it's for our "needs," not, as I heard someone say, for our "greeds." Even in the Lord's Prayer we are asking for the basics, "our daily bread." James, Paul, and Jesus are teaching us to pray for sustenance, not opulence, though the Lord may certainly bless us beyond that if he knows that would be good for us and bring glory to him.

The privilege is ours to approach the throne of grace asking God to supply our needs out of his riches in glory, yet it is here we can run into trouble. For having asked, we sometimes find ourselves questioning when and how, or even if, God will supply.

When You're in a Hurry and God Isn't

Let's be honest: there are times you have asked, maybe even prayed a long time about something and the answer never seemed to come. I know I have. You ask God to save a failing marriage, to deliver a friend's child from an addiction, to heal a terminally ill loved-one. You sincerely seek him to help you sell a house or find a job, to give you clear guidance on a decision, to supply a financial need. You ask him—frequently and fervently—to fix a fractured friendship or to work in the life of a loved one so they will become interested in knowing the Lord. You know your request is not only a good one, you are convinced it must be God's will. So, you pray for it, plead for it, maybe for a long time. You keep telling yourself God is powerful enough to do anything. With him nothing is impossible. You pray on, but nothing happens. You try to trust, but you doubt. Maybe he doesn't hear you, or if so, maybe he really doesn't care, or maybe he isn't as powerful as you thought.

You think of stories you've heard of people praying for things, like the Ramundos and our McDonald's McMiracle, and of God

---

[34] James 4:3.

providing, oftentimes remarkably. If you've heard of him, you think of the stories of George Mueller, the legendary giant of prayer who ran orphanages in England in the 1800s. Caring for thousands of children and hiring a large staff, he prayed about every need every day. He told no one but God, and God came through every time. Every. Single. Time. One morning Mueller had no milk, prayed for it, and right at breakfast time, with the children already sitting around the tables, a dairyman's wagon broke down right in front of the orphanage dining hall. Knowing the milk would soon spoil, he gave it to Mueller and the children had their breakfast.

Things like that happened to Mueller all the time! "Well, good for him," you say, a touch of sarcasm in your voice, "it's not happening for me that way." So you conclude that compared to George Mueller and so many other folks you've heard about, you're either a spiritual midget or God can't do for you what he did for them. You quit asking—for days, weeks, maybe months—only to feel guilty for doubting. You remember God wants you to present your needs to him, so you ask him to forgive your disillusionment driven doubting and with renewed vigor press on, bringing your request to him once more.

You may be struggling with prayer that way now, and that's the way it is sometimes. It's a reality my wife and I have struggled with from time to time. And when that happens, Noni and I have learned to remind each other of what Jesus says to do when the answer doesn't come. Pray on. Don't quit. Press on.

Jesus tells a parable in Luke 11 and another one in Luke 18 to illustrate how we "should always pray and never give up."[35] He tells us not to lose heart but to take heart and keep on praying, keep on asking, keep on seeking, and keep on knocking. Keep on keeping on! Don't give up, give in, or give out. That's what "the Mrs. and me" do, and we have never been sorry we did.

---

[35] Luke 18:1.

Still, how do we deal with it when God doesn't respond as quickly as we wish he would or think he should? I heard a fellow pastor fume one time, "My problem with prayer is that I'm always in a hurry and God isn't!"

Sometimes the winning is in the waiting. God may not be withholding his answer as much as getting us ready for it. God's timeline is different from ours and our having to wait may actually be preparing us for his plans and purposes for us. With God, something is happening even when nothing is happening.

Prolific Christian author Robert Morgan weighs in on this when he writes, "It takes time to align all the circumstances for the best outcome. It takes time for faith to develop and deepen. It takes time for the human heart to soften or heal. So, keep praying, and wait patiently for him."[36]

While God is preparing your heart to receive the answer, you think you're waiting on him, when in reality, he's waiting on you. He may be taking his sweet old time because he wants to make some changes in your life, possibly even some that have nothing to do with what you're asking him for! Yes, "Prayer changes things," as the old adage goes, but prayer also changes you. In those cases, when the changes come, the answer may quickly follow. Just think, the very thing you're praying for him to change might be the very thing he wants to use to change you! That means he's not about to remove it until the job is done.

When you don't receive an answer as quickly as you'd like, it gives you time to clarify what you really need and should be asking for. Many of our prayers are so vague and general we wouldn't recognize the answer it if hit us in the face. Waiting gives you time to think it through, be specific, search for scripture that sheds light on it, refine and refocus the request, modify it, change or clarify it, and maybe even decide if you need it badly enough

---

[36] Robert Morgan, "September 21," in *My All in All* (Nashville, TN: B&H Publishing Group, 2008).

to keep praying for it. Maybe God is testing you to see how much you really yearn for the riches in glory you're seeking.

Another thing to consider is that when we're in a hurry and God isn't, the delayed answer to prayer can be a faith-strengthener. It takes faith to pray, and faith, like a muscle, gets bigger and stronger when it's worked and stretched.

I wonder how many times I have missed a blessing, forfeited the answer to prayer God was willing and waiting to give, because I stopped short. I threw in the towel, quit praying, gave out, and lost out. God's timetable is usually different, *and slower*, than ours. He is operating on his "a day is like a thousand years … and a thousand years is like a day" timetable, so "The Lord isn't really being slow about his promise, as some people think."[37]

After Jesus's ascension, his disciples gathered 120 of his followers in compliance with his command they stay and pray until the Holy Spirit empowered them to be the church and do God's work. Jesus's mother and brothers were among them. I can imagine how it might have gone. They started praying on a Thursday—delighted, excited, and ignited at the prospect of the promised power. All day long they prayed but nothing happened. Same thing Friday and Saturday. Except for a short business meeting to pick a successor to Judas, they kept at their task of praying and seeking.

Then came Sunday. Surely *this* is the day. After all, his followers reminded each other, that's when Jesus rose from the dead. Yes, Sunday—this is the perfect day for the Lord to send the Holy Spirit. But nothing. Nada. Zip, zilch, zero.

Come Monday, they have to send someone to the grocery store for more food. They hadn't planned on it taking this long.

Weary, the group presses prayerfully on.

Sometime Tuesday morning, Thomas turns to Philip as they take a break to grab some coffee and donuts and says, "You know,

---

[37] 2 Peter 3:8–9.

Phil, I'm starting to have some doubts. If this Holy Spirit were coming, don't you think he would have been here by now? Maybe we misunderstood what Jesus meant?"

"Yes, you may have a point," Philip responds. "Say, hand me the cream and sugar, will ya?"

Still they slogged on—into Wednesday—through Thursday—on to Friday. Then came Saturday, the tenth day, and all heaven broke loose. The wind of the Spirit blew, the fire of the Spirit fell, the church was born, the lost were saved, the book of Acts was launched, and the Christian faith charged into the centuries. After ten days of praying.

But what if they had stopped praying after nine days? They would have been on the verge of God's answer and blessing, not known it, and missed it.

I've heard people say, "God is never in a hurry but always on time." That expresses the greater truth that God's delays are not necessarily God's denials. Instead, they are his perfect timing for our greater good and his greatest glory. In this sense, his delays are blessings in disguise. Just ask Mary and Martha about the Lord not responding to their 911 call and racing to Bethany the minute he heard their brother, his good friend Lazarus, was gravely ill.[38] Anxiously, they went to the door and looked down the road again and again. No Jesus. Lazarus was sinking—fast. Still no Jesus. It went on like this for days and they would mutter to each other, "Where is Jesus? When is he going to get here? He did miracles for so many others. Where is he now that *we* need him?"

Lazarus dies.

When Jesus shows up four days after the funeral, an ever-petulant take-charge Martha reminds him that but for his dilly-dallying, her brother would still be alive: "Lord, if only you had been here, my brother would not have died."[39] A moment later,

---

[38] John 11:4–7.
[39] John 11:21.

Mary, the normally chilled out type-B personality of the duo, reminds the Lord his slow response has cost them their brother.[40] But Jesus makes it clear to her, the disciples, and anybody else paying attention that he's got something better up his sleeve, which is, as it turns out, to raise Lazarus from the dead.

The next time you question why God is taking so long to answer your prayer, you might want to consider the possibility he's got something even better in mind. Think of it in terms of a time you ordered something online or through the mail where the order form included a note that said, "If we are out of this item, we reserve the right to substitute one of equal or greater value." When we pray, God reserves the right to substitute an answer of equal or greater value!

There is another way God may reserve the right to answer our prayer at a later time than we would wish. A story that never fails to encourage me is told by an 18th century church leader, Benjamin Titus Roberts. Here it is, in his own words:

> A dying minister said: "I feel happy and assured of my salvation, as a poor, lost sinner, saved through a Saviour's precious, atoning blood." But there seemed to be something weighing upon his mind. One inquired, "My dear brother, is there anything that is now a cause of anxiety to you?" The dying man put his hand under his pillow, and drew out a piece of paper, on which were written the names of twenty-five unconverted, leading men of his parish, and with tears he said: "Yes, there is one cause of anxiety, and here it is: it is the salvation of these twenty-five men. I have prayed much for these twenty-five men, name by name. If I could know that these men would be converted, I

---

[40] John 11:32.

could then say, 'Lord, now let thy servant depart in peace, for mine eyes have seen thy salvation.'" With this great burden upon his heart, he died.

Sometime after his death, at an ecclesiastical gathering, his successor was inquired of about these men. With much feeling he replied, "Brethren every one of these twenty-five men has been converted. We believe they were converted in answer to the prayer of our sainted brother." "The effectual fervent prayer of a righteous man availeth much" (James 5:16).[41]

What a wonderful thought: Some of those heartfelt prayers we have offered again and again, may go on being answered after, perhaps long after, we've gone to heaven.

When God's Answer Is No ... Or Worse than No

A long-time-coming answer to prayer is one thing, but when God's answer is "No," or what sometimes seems worse than "No," that's another matter. Is he hoarding those riches in glory?

My mother, who like *her* mother, my grandmother, was a prayer warrior if there ever was one, taught me a valuable lesson one day when I was a teenager and let her know I had a beef with God. I had needed an answer to prayer and he hadn't come through. I made the mistake of referring to it as an "unanswered prayer." Mom spoke up. "Oh, he answered it alright," she told me. Incredulous, I responded, "If he answered it, wouldn't I know it?"

---

[41] B.T. Roberts, *Fishers of Men* (Indianapolis, IN: Light and Life Communications, 2007), 202–203.

"Son," my mother said softly, "he did answer it. His answer was no. After all, no *is* an answer. He loves you, wants what's best for you, and when your request is for something he, in his infinite wisdom knows will prove wrong for you, you want him to say no, don't you?"

Since no is an answer, it is correct, then, to say there is no such thing as "unanswered prayer." The only prayers that go unanswered are the prayers that go unoffered.

Mom went home to heaven not long ago at the age of ninety-eight. I am certain God is still answering prayers she offered when she was here, but thanks to her I have grown to appreciate no as an answer. I am glad that when I pray for something that is not right or good for me, my God answers no.

As Jesus is teaching about prayer, he offers the following illustration in the Sermon on the Mount to his congregation:

> You parents—if your children ask for a loaf of bread, do you give them a stone instead? Or if they ask for a fish, do you give them a snake? Of course not! So, if you sinful people know how to give good gifts to your children, how much more will your heavenly Father give good gifts to those who ask him.[42]

One implication of our Lord's teaching in these verses is that the heavenly Father always gives gifts to his children that will be good for them—never bad. When God denies a request we make of him, it is because he knows whatever we are asking for is bad for us, whether we can see it at the time or not. No doubt there have been times I was asking for something I thought was good, not realizing it would turn out to be a stone or a snake. God, wanting to give only good gifts to me, said no.

---

[42] Matthew 7:9–11.

The very fact we question God when his answer is no, or even just slow, betrays a wrong belief on our part that we have the right to always know exactly what God is doing and why he is doing it. As if he answers to us! That's just not possible, and for good reason. We learn in Isaiah that his thoughts are nothing like our thoughts, and his ways are far beyond anything we can even begin to imagine. Just as the heavens are higher than the earth, so are his ways higher than our ways and his thoughts higher than ours.[43] Others scriptures sound the same note.

God has a whole different way of looking at things than we do. His value system is entirely different from ours. Our earth-bound temporal minds cannot conceive or perceive what he's about from his eternal perspective. He knows what he's doing even when it doesn't look like it to us. When it seems he is ignoring us, or maybe even being outright cruel, he is actually being neither. To think that of him is either a terrible misunderstanding on our part or a lie of the devil we have fallen for. Satan, you recall, is the prince of prevaricators, his first weapon of choice the lie.

The Bible also makes it clear that some of the hard stuff we would pray away, God allows to toughen us up. Paul tells us problems and trials produce endurance, which builds character, which in turn strengthens hope.[44] James, the brother of Jesus, sounds the same note when he tells us trials and the testing of our faith produce an endurance that leads to maturity.[45] Paul and James make me wonder if, before we ask God to relieve us of the trial or difficulty, we should first ask him how he wants to use it to build character, strengthen hope, produce endurance, and grow maturity in us?

I have heard it suggested that one of the reasons God doesn't spare us all the tough stuff in this life is that it makes us hungry

---

[43] Isaiah 55:8–9.
[44] Romans 5:3–4.
[45] James 1:2–4.

for heaven, where everything will be perfect. If all were bliss for the believer in this life, why look forward to heaven? That take on it may not be convincing to you, and that's OK, but it is a thought that has brought comfort to many a Christ-follower.

It is the nature of a book like this to include stories of God's wonderful provision in response to prayer, and this one does that. But where are the accounts of the times God's answer is no, and because of that someone is left to deal with disappointment and disillusionment; those times when a believer feels let down or even betrayed by God?

The last paper I wrote in college, just before heading off to pastor my first church while starting seminary, was titled "The Problem of God." Not that God is a problem. That was the term used in our philosophy texts and classes for the difficulty of accounting for the existence of a good and all-powerful God in the face of evil and suffering in our world. I was challenged by the undertaking, and the challenge has proven ongoing throughout my life and ministry.

When God Doesn't Make Sense

It's true: God can be tough to figure out at times. OK, he is downright impossible to figure out a lot of the time. One of my all-time favorite professors was Paul E. Little, who at the time I took a class from him at Trinity Evangelical Divinity School was assistant to the president of Inter-Varsity Christian Fellowship. The author of several books, his most popular work is the evangelism classic *How to Give Away Your Faith*. Greatly gifted at interacting with college and grad students in or out of class, he was transparent, engaging, humorous, and exhibited a contagious faith.

A couple years after I was in Paul Little's class and had transferred to another seminary, the periodical *Moody Monthly* published an article he had written titled "The God Who Never

Lets Things Just Happen." I read it, clipped it out, and it was still lying on my desk when, a few weeks later, I heard the news Paul Little had just been killed in a car accident. He was in his midforties. After the initial shock waves rolled over me, with tears in my eyes, I reached again for his article, now reading it with a whole new perspective.

Like I said, God can be tough to figure. But in that article, my old prof had left a helpful word behind. He noted that God is sovereign, in control, he never lets things just happen, not even what is, from our perspective, a tragic accident. When answers are in short supply, he wrote, that supreme truth can be reassuring. Then, Professor Little brought it all home in the last two sentences of his article, stating, "Nothing happens by accident. And we can rest with confidence in that."[46]

You pray for a loved-one's safety as they travel. "Father, grant them traveling mercies." The next day the phone rings. There was a car accident (or plane crash, or train wreck, or bus incident, fill in the blank). No survivors. "But Lord, I thought you'd ..."

You beg God to heal a five-year-old of cancer. You plead, you cry, you fast, you beg, you enlist fellow believers everywhere in the effort. But one day you attend a funeral, heartbroken. And as you stare at a small, white casket your heart cries, "Why, Father? Surely you could have ..."

Think of all the things you pray about that God can and sometimes does, but not always, unleash a miracle on: a grandson with leukemia, an infertile couple desperate for a child, an abusive parent or spouse, a failing business, an old college buddy dealing with deep depression and thoughts of suicide. My list of hypotheticals could go on, but like you, I've had my own stuff to deal with.

For months Noni and I prayed the child we were expecting, our second, would be born healthy. You know, ten fingers, ten

---

[46] Paul Little, "The God Who Never Lets Things Just Happen," *Moody Monthly*, June 1975, 42–44.

toes, and all that. It didn't matter if the baby was a boy or a girl (this was back in prehistoric times before ultrasound let you know the gender long before the birth). Besides, we agreed with the expression that, "It's not important that you get what you want, just so you want what you get." And what we wanted and prayed for was a healthy child.

After the early morning birth, I picked up three-year-old Theresa at the neighbors', informed her she had a healthy baby brother, and her mother and I were naming him after two Bible characters, Samuel Mark. Then, the two of us went out on a daddy-daughter date to celebrate over breakfast. As we ate, the nickname "Sam the Man" just popped up and seemed perfect. After breakfast, we went out and bought "Sam the Man" a baseball-themed sleeper. I knew he was destined for great things on the ball field.

Eight days later our healthy son perished in his sleep, a victim of sudden infant death syndrome, better known as "crib death." The devastation seemed more than we could bear. We went from rejoicing that God had answered our prayer for a healthy baby, to the shock of his passing. Underscoring our happiness turned to hurt, cards congratulating us on our new baby were still coming in the mail mingled with sympathy cards for his passing.

From the day our daughters were born, Noni and I prayed nearly every day for the men they would one day marry, that they would know and serve the Lord and be good and loving husbands. Yes was the answer when daughter number one married, and twenty-some years later that has proven wonderfully true.

When our second daughter married a man preparing for the ministry, the Lord had again honored our prayers—or so we thought. But it didn't take long to see he was not the man we had prayed for all those years, culminating in his betrayal of her. But had God betrayed *us*? I mean, twenty-seven years of praying for a devoted follower of Christ for us to entrust our dear daughter to and look what she got. Why keep praying the same thing for our grandchildren?

Both personal experiences I have just related weren't only no answers to prayer, they seemed worse than no, since both appeared to have been answered yes before the rug got pulled out from under us. In some ways, the death of our daughter's marriage seemed worse than the death of our son, except by then many more years of walking with the Lord had taught us that we're not always going to know what God's up to, but we'll trust him just the same.

On the other hand, we ought not too quickly conclude a prayer has not been answered as we had hoped, even when it appears that way. For years the Christians in my wife's family prayed for her father to come to trust and know Christ. A veteran of both the Second World War and the Korean War, "Sarge," as he was known, died at sixty-eight years of age. At his death, he had still not taken that step of faith leading to salvation. Twenty-five years after his passing, at a conference we were attending, my wife and one of her sisters came upon a pastor who had known their father. As they talked, this pastor reminisced warmly about visiting their dad just prior to his going to the hospital for major surgery. Sarge would die a few days after the operation. But the pastor explained how during that visit he had shared the gospel, and Master Sergeant Alexander Graz had most definitely committed his life to Christ. It took a quarter of a century for them to know, but that day tears of joy flowed freely from two happy daughters.

The Fiery Furnace Clause

Noni and I often include what we call "the fiery furnace clause" in our praying. It comes from the story of Shadrach, Meshach, and Abednego in the third chapter of the Old Testament's book of Daniel. I had an aunt whose memory crutch for their names was "Shake the Bed, Make the Bed, and to Bed We Go"!

The three lads, among the Hebrews in captivity in Babylon, refused to bow down and worship an idol made of gold that King Nebuchadnezzar had set up. When they were dragged before the king, he gave them one more chance, then he told them if they refused, they'd be pitched into a blazing furnace.

The reply of the three to the king infuriated him. "Threaten us all you want, but the God we serve is perfectly capable of delivering us, and he will rescue us. *But if not*, let there be no doubt in your mind, we will still serve him."[47]

If you know the story, you know the ticked-off king had the furnace stoked seven times hotter than usual—so hot the soldiers who pushed Shadrach, Meshach, and Abednego into the roaring flames were killed by it! The three of *them* however, protected by a fourth man in the fire, the Son of God, did not perish in the inferno. In fact, scripture tells us not so much as a hair on their heads was singed, their clothing wasn't scorched, and afterward they didn't even smell of smoke!

As I write this, Noni and I are praying daily for healing for seventeen people we know who are battling cancer. When we pray for them, we almost always include the "fiery furnace clause": "Lord, we know you are able to deliver them, but if not, we will still trust in you."

Paul prayed that his "thorn in the flesh" would be removed. The answer was "No," though God gave him the grace and power to deal with it.[48] In Gethsemane's garden, Jesus prayed that the cup of the cross with its suffering, humiliation, sin-bearing, and death, would be removed from him. Hebrews 5:7 adds to the record in the gospels, telling us, "He offered prayers and pleadings, with a loud cry and tears, to the one who could rescue him from death." The answer to his prayer was "No," for our salvation's sake.[49] Both

---

[47] Daniel 3:17–18, author's paraphrase.
[48] 2 Corinthians 12:7–10.
[49] Matthew 26:39; Mark 14:36; Luke 22:42.

the Savior and the apostle bowed without question to the will of the Father.

There are times we pray when God's answer is, "Yes, I'm glad you asked." There are times his answer is, "No, I have a better idea!" Other times the answer might be, "Yes, but not yet." Still other times his answer is, "Yes, and here's even more!" And then there are those times, as Mom taught me, God's answer is, "No, I love you too much." And there are even times that put our faith to the test, when the answer is, "No, and it is going to hurt deeply, but it can't be explained to you now."

Joey and his younger brother Keith were in the first church I pastored. Both boys were afflicted with muscular dystrophy. In recent years medical science has made much progress in dealing with this illness. Today the sufferer has the potential to graduate from high school, go to college, pursue a career, get married, and have children. Back when this story takes place, for junior-higher Joey and middle-grades Keith, the prognosis was grim. They were not expected to live past their teen years. For that reason, intercession on their behalf was constantly offered at church, in prayer groups, and in the homes of our people. Faithfully we prayed for a miracle of healing.

Joey and Keith's parents were separated, so, along with their younger sister they came to church every week with Grandpa and Grandma Olson. Grandpa Olson was Keith's best buddy and hero. Grandpa, as cheerful a chap as you'll find, was the one bright spot in the life of a boy whose home and body were falling apart. But one day further tragedy struck. Grandpa, who had seemed in the peak of health, died, felled by a massive heart attack.

We continued as we always had, praying for Keith's and his brother's healing. Then, within a few weeks of his grandfather's funeral, Keith was diagnosed with bone cancer. It seemed that the answer to our prayers for healing was not only no, but now it felt even worse than no.

Come the day Keith was to have his right arm amputated in an attempt to check the spread of the disease, I drove to the hospital with a heavy heart to pray with this ten-year-old before surgery. As I finished praying, in spite of my resolve to be strong for Keith's sake, tears trickled down my cheeks. My little friend looked up and caught me crying. Then, he flashed his heartwarming smile my way and exclaimed, "Please don't worry, Pastor Tom. Me and God can handle *anything!*"

A few months later, on the same day I had a wedding of all things, I officiated at Keith's funeral.

Fifty years have come and gone since the day a young boy took me to school and taught me how you handle it when God says no: with childlike trust.

> Trust him when dark thoughts assail thee,
> Trust him when thy faith is small,
> Trust him when simply to trust him,
> Is the hardest thing of all.
> —Childhood poem

CHAPTER FIVE

The Spirit of God Enabling Us

And the Holy Spirit helps us in our weakness. For example,
we don't know what God wants us to pray for. But the
Holy Spirit prays for us with groanings that cannot be
expressed in words. And the Father who knows all hearts
knows what the Spirit is saying, for the Spirit pleads
for us believers in harmony with God's own will.

ROMANS 8:26–27

Those two verses! Are they cool or what? Read them again. Go ahead. Maybe a little slower this time.

I don't know about you, but sometimes I'm just not smart enough to know how to pray, or even what to pray, about some things. And that's where the Holy Spirit comes in.

Daniel Boone, famous pioneer, explorer, and frontiersman, was asked: "Have you ever been lost?" Boone replied, "No, I've never been lost, but I have been bewildered a few times; sometimes for days and once for a whole week." The Holy Spirit is there for those times we find ourselves bewildered in prayer. He rides to the rescue, sometimes speaking *to* us, other times speaking *for* us.

The Holy Spirit Speaks *to* Us

The best illustration I know of the Spirit speaking to us to inform, direct, and guide our praying along the lines of God's will, comes from the book *Experiencing God*, by Henry Blackaby. He writes:

> For his sixth birthday, my oldest son Richard was old enough to have a bicycle. I looked all around for a bicycle. I found a blue Schwinn. I bought it and hid it in the garage. Then I had a task—to convince Richard that he needed a blue Schwinn bike. For the next little while, we began to work with Richard. Richard decided that what he really wanted for his birthday was a blue Schwinn bike. Do you know what Richard got? Well, the bike was already in the garage. I just had to convince him to ask for it. He asked for it, and he got it!

> What happens when you pray? The Holy Spirit knows what God has "in the garage." It is already there. The Holy Spirit's task is to get you to want it—to get you to ask for it. What will happen when you ask for things God already wants to give or do? You will always receive it. Why? Because you have asked *according to the will of God*.[50]

One of the roles the Holy Spirit plays in the prayer life of the believer, as illustrated by Blackaby's story, is to speak to us, revealing the will of God so we can pray accordingly. How does the

---

[50] Henry T. Blackaby and Claude V. King, *Experiencing God* (Nashville, TN: Broadman & Holman Publishers, 1994), 110-111. Another excellent book by Blackaby on this subject, this one coauthored with his son, Richard, is *Hearing God's Voice* (Nashville, TN: Broadman & Holman Publishers, 2002).

Spirit do that? For me it is usually through an impression he brings to my mind and heart that is unmistakable and accompanied by a sense of certainty. Others claim he leads them, at least occasionally, in an audible voice. Sometimes the Spirit shows a believer through circumstances what the will of God is that they might pray for it, and other times it may come through the wise, godly counsel of another believer.

There are other ways than those just mentioned that the Spirit helps a believer discern the will of the Father, but what do you do if he hasn't given you any direction? How do you even pray about that concern or need?

The Holy Spirit Speaks *for* Us

There are those times when the Spirit hasn't shown us directly and clearly what to pray for. And this is where the two verses at the start of this chapter, Romans 8:26–27, come into play.

With those two verses in mind, here's how I like to think of it. I am praying about something that burdens my heart and befuddles my mind. It may be a heavy, even heartbreaking concern, for another person, perhaps a loved one, or it may be a personal need or hurt. But the words that stammer out of my mouth betray all the confusion in my mind. I don't know how to pray about it. It isn't that I haven't tried. In fact, I have, and now I'm all prayed out. It is then the Holy Spirit looks at me and with compassion says, "Look at Thomas there. He means well and is trying so hard, but he just doesn't get it. I'd better help him out. So, here's what I'm going to do. I'm going to take all that muddle in his mind, and all that hurt in his heart, and all that confusion in his prayers, and turn it all into the perfect prayer request completely in harmony with the will of God and present it before the Father on his behalf."

Isn't that what Paul is saying? And isn't that wonderful beyond words?

Eugene Peterson captures the idea well in his rendering of verse 26 in *The Message*: "The moment we get tired in the waiting, God's Spirit is right alongside helping us along. If we don't know how or what to pray, it doesn't matter. He does our praying in and for us, making prayer out of our wordless sighs, our aching groans."

Whether the following story is true, or the product of someone's fertile imagination, I'm not sure, but either way it makes a good point.

A little girl sat in the back row at church while her parents joined the rest of the congregation up front for a prayer meeting. She sat quietly with her coloring book and crayons, filling in the pictures.

Meanwhile, the adults were enjoying a lengthy time of prayer, one after the other speaking to God. They uttered lofty words of worship for a transcendentally awesome God, lifted prayers of thanksgiving for his beneficent and bountiful blessings, and for his provisions for previous petitions. They called upon him to open the windows of heaven and pour out his immeasurable mercy and grace upon them. Listening to their litany of linguistics, the little girl could not understand even a little of what they were saying, but she knew they were talking to God and that was a good thing.

As the prayer meeting progressed, there came a silence of several seconds in between prayers. Seizing the moment, the little girl stood up on her back pew and called out loudly, "Dear God: A, B, C, D, E, F, G," and on through the alphabet she went until she finished with a flourish, "W, X, Y, Z, Amen!" With that, she plopped back down.

The startled congregation, their reverent attitude shattered, could not believe what had just happened, and they turned and watched as the mother ran back to her daughter. "Honey, what are you doing? Can't you see we're trying to pray up there?" "Oh, Mommy," the little girl said, "I know. I was too. But I don't know how to talk to God with all those big words, so I thought

I'd just give him the letters and let him put them together the way he wants to."

When we yearn to connect with God but can't even make sense of our thoughts, let alone put them into words, that's when the Holy Spirit is available to move in, take over, and put the words together the way he wants to.

All along, then, whether we are confused about how to pray or whether the pathway of our praying is crystal clear, it is the Holy Spirit who imparts to our lives and implants in our hearts gifts of faith and trust, so that we might wholeheartedly seek the Giver for the gifts he would give.

Christian Atheists

Before we even begin to pray in confidence with the Spirit's help, some of us may need to let the Spirit strengthen and build the muscles of our faith.

When my daughters, Theresa and Christy, were teenagers, they had a joke they loved to tell. It was about a Christian who left home for his freshman year at the state university and found himself rooming with an atheist. One day the atheist challenged the Christian. "I'm going to prove to you there is no God," he announced, "and I'll use the perfect proof, your own 5 senses. First," he began, "can you see God?"

"No," the Christian replied.

"Can you hear God?"

"No," he said again.

"Can you taste God?"

"No."

"Can you smell God?"

"No."

"Can you feel God?" Here, the Christian stopped him. "Yes! Sometimes I can feel God—in my heart."

"Well, there you have it," summed up the atheist, "with your own senses I have just proved four out of five, there is no God."

"Well wait just a minute, my learned friend," the Christian said, "using your own logic, answer me this. Can you see your brain?"

"No," the atheist said.

"Can you hear it?"

"No."

"Taste it?"

"No."

"Even smell it?"

"No."

"And finally, can you feel it?"

"No."

"So, there *you* have it, the Christian declared, "using your own logic, five out of five, you have no brain!"

If you're reading this book, especially if you've made it this far, it is likely you are not an atheist. But I wonder, is it possible to be a *practical* if not a *practicing* atheist? By that I mean claiming to know and to have a great big God with tremendous resources and wondrous riches, who loves you and cares about you, yet living as if he is puny, powerless, and poor by not bringing your needs to him and trusting him to meet them?

Perhaps, then, the place many of us can start growing our confidence in God and building-up our trust muscles is by asking for the Holy Spirit to wing our way the gift of faith that we might truly believe—freely, boldly, consistently, and continually bringing our requests to the Father.

Real Prayer Is Really (*Really*) Hard Work

There is another way the Holy Spirit helps us when we pray. Much of the time prayer can be just plain hard work, and we need the encouragement and energy the Spirit will bring to our prayer life. Too many believers seem to feel since prayer is talking to God, it should be, to use a favorite expression of a friend of mine, "easy peasy." When it takes more mental focus, physical stamina, and spiritual resources than they figured it would, they grow discouraged and give up.

The rigors of sincere, intense, persistent prayer, made exponentially more demanding by the length of the passage of time we must pray about some things, can be physically, emotionally, and spiritually exhausting in every way. Sometimes on Sunday mornings when I would remind people of our midweek prayer service and invite them to come, I would do something any pastor reading this will find incomprehensible. I would wrap up my invitation by saying, "But some of you shouldn't come. Prayer can be just plain hard work, and you're not ready for it. If you're not committed to facing the hard work of praying, please do yourself a favor and stay home."

I needed to tell them that because our prayer meetings were all prayer and nothing but prayer. We didn't call it a "prayer meeting," and then have forty minutes of Bible study, fifteen minutes of sharing prayer requests, and then a five-minute lick-and-a-promise prayer at the end. No, we had small groups and classes for Bible study and sharing. Prayer meeting was prayer meeting. Rarely did we even begin by sharing prayer requests. We just started right in, praying. When someone had a prayer request or something else they thought we ought to pray about, they didn't tell it to everybody, they told it to God, and then others followed up by praying about it too. And so it would go for sixty or seventy minutes, maybe more, of concerted effort.

Yes, prayer is hard work, but the Holy Spirit is there to fill our tank with the gas we need to reach our destination. He is the energizer who fills us and thrills us with the vigor to push on, if we will invite him in and turn him loose.

The Stops between Our Steps

Some time ago, the *Detroit Free Press* published an interesting article about why a pigeon walks the way it does, with those herky-jerky head movements. Because it cannot adjust its focus while moving, the pigeon has to bring its head to a complete stop between steps in order to refocus. With every step it takes, it is head forward, stop and focus, head back, stop and focus, head forward, stop and focus—well, you get the idea.

In the Christian walk we have the same problem as the pigeon. We have a hard time keeping things in focus and seeing where we're going. We too need to make some stops between our steps to see clearly. Regular prayer times are those stops, and the Holy Spirit is there to help us focus on what we need to see. Thus the importance of our daily rendezvous at the throne of grace. The Spirit is present to meet with us, minister to us, and help us anticipate and navigate the difficulties and opportunities before us. He's there to guide, guard, and govern our everyday walk.

> The work of intercessors is a lot
> like working for the phone company.
> Some days we dig holes. Some days
> we plant poles. Some days we string
> wire. And some days we make contact!
> —B. J. Willhite

The People of God Enfolding Us

Pray in the Spirit at all times and on every occasion. Stay alert and be persistent in your prayers for all believers everywhere.

EPHESIANS 6:18

The church is the army that marches on its knees. As God's people pray for each other, we enfold one another and others in the power of prayer.

I have been a part of church world my whole life. I started attending church nine months before I was born. I'm like the fella who said, "I had a drug problem when I was young. I was drug to church on Sunday mornings. I was drug to church on Sunday evenings. I was drug to church for midweek kids' club and youth group, and any other time the doors were open. Those drugs are still in my veins and I don't want to ever kick the habit."

On top of that, during my growing-up years, our family's closest friends were our church friends, and we socialized with them often. And if my seven-plus decades of experience in the church have shown me anything, it is that God's people know how to be obedient to Paul's call in Ephesians 6:18 to pray for believers everywhere.

Praying for one another is one of the things Christians do best and most often, something I would come to appreciate more than ever in April 2016.

April 1, 2016, began the way nearly every morning had for me for years: Rise at five a.m., do some core and strength exercises, go for a long run followed by breakfast, take a shower, then dress, and go to work. But on this day, shoes laced-up and ready to run, I could not get started. I had the worse sore throat and earache of my life. And then the chills set in. When I say chills, I'm talking bone-jarring, teeth-chattering, body-racking chills.

I went back to the bedroom, stumbling around and waking up my wife. Startled from sleep, Noni said, "You're not done already?"

"No," I told her, "I haven't even started. I feel awful. Got the chills. Gonna take a hot shower and see if that helps."

A few minutes later, I staggered still shaking back into the bedroom and told her, "I've got to go to the emergency room *right now.*" I needed to say no more. After a lifetime of resisting any suggestion I see a doctor for any reason, the fact I was actually volunteering to seek medical attention convinced her something was definitely wrong. She was wide awake, fully dressed, car keys in hand, and ready to drive in a matter of minutes.

By the time we arrived at the hospital, just minutes from our home, I was completely out of it and was admitted with a severe case of influenza. I was totally dehydrated, had double pneumonia, the lining of my heart was inflamed, and my entire system was poisoned with sepsis. My body was under attack by an army of viral and bacterial terrorists. The night before, I considered myself the healthiest sixty-seven-year-old I knew and went to bed feeling just fine. Now, a matter of hours later, I was fighting for my life.

My second night in the hospital, I had a heart attack. I don't remember much, but Noni says within seconds my room was crowded with medical personnel—doctors, nurses, respiratory therapists, EKG techs, and more—ten in all. Let me throw in a little suggestion here: If you're thinking about having a heart attack, you might want to think about having it at a hospital.

It took the medical staff a few hours to get me stabilized and move me to the cardiac care unit, where the battle to get my oxygen up to an acceptable level continued well into the next day. In fact, they were getting ready to put me on a ventilator when things finally took a turn for the better.

A couple days later, a heart catheterization revealed I had nine blockages—yes, you read that right—nine blockages in my coronary arteries—eight of them from ninety to one hundred percent. The heart's remarkable ability to produce four collateral arteries serving as natural bypasses, a benefit of years of running, had been keeping me going for who knows how long—that and the grace of God.

Two weeks of nursing me through the flu, pneumonia, and sepsis, running endless tests, dealing with internal bleeding, and a cluster of cascading complications followed. Then they performed open heart surgery, a triple bypass, followed by more complications, several blood transfusions, days of delirium, nights filled with hallucinations, and an out-of-whack heart rhythm that defied resolution. Finally, after nearly a month in the hospital, I was headed home for what would be a long but good recovery.

In that month in the hospital, and even before I was fully cognizant of all that was happening to me, I knew God's people were caring for my family and praying for me. Most of the time I was there, I could not have visitors except for family. Nor was I capable of reading the cards people were sending. But even without the reassurance that comes from cards and visitors, I instinctively knew believers everywhere were doing the loving yet hard work of praying for me.

Church prayer chains were set in motion. Phones rang, and the word went out, calling people to pray. Prayer meetings, small groups, and Bible studies spoke with the Lord on my behalf.

Solitary figures knelt in quiet corners of their homes in early morning hours to intercede for me. Couples and families gathered around the dinner table presented my needs at the throne of grace. Ministers included me as they led their congregations in Sunday morning prayers. And thanks to the marvels of social media, the call to prayer was transmitted across the country and around the world, reaching even to friends I had not seen since high school nearly fifty years before.

God's people were bombarding heaven from every corner of the country and all around the globe, interceding on my behalf. If you have seen it, picture the opening scene of that great movie *It's a Wonderful Life*, with all those prayers for a desperate George Bailey flying into heaven like missiles.

When I was finally able to read all the cards and notes people sent with expressions of concern, love, encouragement, and prayer, the most special of all were the handmade cards from children at my church. Not long before, I had done a children's sermon wearing GAP brand clothing and cap, suggesting we should let the three letters of that name remind us that God Answers Prayer. Scribbled somewhere on nearly every one of their homemade cards, youngsters had included the initials "GAP."

How wonderful to be prayed for. And right along with that and maybe even better, how wonderful to lift others up in prayer. The prophet Samuel not only saw it as a privilege to intercede on behalf of others, he considered it a mandate. When the people of Israel pleaded for his prayers, the crusty old codger responded, "As for me, I vow that I will not sin against the Lord by ceasing to pray for you."[51]

In Acts 12, the church gathered, enfolding an imprisoned Peter in their prayers. In response, God dispatched an angel to pull off a divine jail break. Of that miracle, the ever-quotable Puritan preacher, Thomas Watson, said, "The angel fetched Peter out of

---

[51] 1 Samuel 12:23 (CSB).

prison, but it was prayer that fetched the angel." Yes, the prayers of God's people.

Throughout my pastoral ministry, I spent Friday afternoons visiting in the homes of senior saints so we could pray together about the needs of those in our church family and other concerns. These were not just "pastoral visits," as they once were called, where I went to their home to read the Bible and pray for them. I was there so we could pray together about God's kingdom, God's people, and God's work. Besides, these seasoned saints were several grades ahead of me in the school of prayer, especially early in my ministry. I needed not only to pray with them, but to learn from them how to pray, and have them pray for me.

When I was leading the midweek prayer ministry called, "The Prayer Force," from time to time I would begin by saying something like, "Tonight we are going to travel through our town, across the country, and around the world. In fact, we are going to visit missionaries and God's work in Africa, South America, Japan, India, and some other countries. And by what marvel are we going to do this? By no marvel except the marvel of prayer. In prayer we'll be there!"

Parents Praying for Their Children

When our verse for this chapter, Ephesians 6:18, instructs Christians to be persistent in praying for all believers everywhere, that includes parents praying for their children. In fact, that's where our prayers ought to start. And there is no statute of limitations on praying for your children. I often jokingly say, "When Noni and I had kids, we thought we were signing up for an eighteen-year enlistment, but eventually we found out it's a life sentence!"

As any Christian parent knows, concern for our children doesn't end just because they're grown and gone from our home. In some ways, it gets even greater. No matter how old our children are, even with families of their own, their hurts and needs still weigh heavily on us, driving us often to our knees. As they mature, there comes a time when we have less influence over them. Through prayer, however, we can still make a big difference in their lives.

One time I closed the door to a little prayer room we have in our home, fell flat on my face, and stayed there an hour and a half weeping and interceding for one of my daughters, who was nearing forty years of age and enduring terrible hurt. Four months later, the fruit of that and other seasons of prayer on her behalf proved to be just what she (and we, her parents) needed.

After thirty-five years as a local church pastor, I was elected superintendent of my denomination's churches in the southern part of our state. When I called my mother, eighty-four years of age at the time, to give her the news, she said, "It never stops with you, you know that?" Not sure what her point was I asked, "What do you mean, Mom?" She replied, "You just never stop giving me reasons to have to keep praying for you." The next story illustrates this point from another perspective.

Doug Campbell's mother was well acquainted with a parent's prayer burden, and she carried it well. When Doug, who has given me permission to tell his story and use his name, was a young man, he had not the slightest inclination toward anything to do with the Lord. He had at the time a job that was an hour's drive from where he lived at home with his mom. Working second shift, every night when he got off work at midnight he would drive twenty minutes, then stop along the way at his favorite "watering hole," as they say. Having had too much to drink, he would climb back in his car and drive the forty minutes the rest of the way home.

In the wee hours of the new morning when Doug finally pulled into his driveway, there would be a light on in the house, and when he entered, he would find his mother sitting at the dining room table. She would welcome him home and then shuffle off to bed.

Years rolled by and this routine continued, Doug often telling his mother she needed her rest and should not wait up for him.

Then, the day came Doug met the Savior. And I mean the guy got 2 Corinthians five-"seventeened"! That's the verse that says, "If anyone is in Christ, he is a new creation; the old has passed away, and see, the new has come."[52] Doug just wasn't the same anymore. He was a new man in Jesus. And it was only then Doug's mother told him the whole story of her staying up night after night.

At the time Doug's mom knew he was getting off work, she would sit down at the table and begin to pray for him. She knew he would be stopping to drink and would end up in no shape to drive. She would beg the Lord to get him home safely. She would pray for others on the highway to be safe as her inebriated son roared down the highway. She would pray that someday before it was too late, Doug would yield to the Savior. And she would keep praying the whole time he was driving until she saw the flash of the headlights on the curtains as he turned into the driveway.

The work of a praying parent is a calling, a trust, and it is never done.

Parents Praying with Their Children

Not only will a Christian parent pray *for* their children, they can pray *with* them as well. Singer-songwriter Robert Hamlet penned a musical tribute to his mother titled "Lady Who Prays for Me." As he was growing up, his mom would pray with her boys every morning as they headed out the door to the school bus stop.

After a young mother heard Hamlet sing his song, she determined to start praying with her own little boy that way. Come the next school day, just before he went out the door, she prayed with him. Five minutes later, he was back with five other

---

[52] Christian Standard Bible.

children from the bus stop in tow. Taken aback, his mother asked what was going on. "The bus was coming," the boy explained, "but their moms didn't pray with them."

When I was in grade school, the pastor of the church our family attended, Ernest Kratzer, told of a time when he was a little boy and their poverty-stricken family was in dire straits. There came a day when they had nothing to eat for supper. Ernie's father had died and his mother was too ill to work outside the home. At dinner time, as they sat together around a table set with empty dishes, his mom said, "Children, let us hold hands and say grace." Little Ernie, fighting back the tears, spoke up. "But Momma, there is no food."

"Just the same," his mother responded, "we will ask God to provide and thank him that he will." With that, she prayed. A few minutes later, the family still gathered around the table staring at empty plates, there came a knock at the door. Ernie ran to answer it and there stood the next-door neighbors, husband and wife, with smiles on their faces, supper in their hands, and a story on their lips about how just a few moments earlier they had both felt strangely and suddenly moved to bring dinner over.

That experience of a mother's trust and a faithful God left a deep and lasting impression on a young boy bound for the ministry.

Men, Man Up!

———

When it comes to praying with and for family, husbands and fathers live under a biblical mandate to serve as priests of their families, and the primary role of a priest is to be an intercessor for those he's responsible for.

Before he went home to heaven in 2002, Edwin Louis Cole was a leader in men's ministries. He has often been called "the father of the Christian men's movement." A compelling leader, dynamic speaker, and prolific writer, just one of his many areas of emphasis and influence was challenging men to be the family priest, praying for and with their wives and children. Ed Cole wrote: "There's a priest in every house. God has designated the man to play the part. Bible student or not, men, you're the priest. Whether you believe it, receive it, live it, or ignore it—you're the priest."[53]

I have this warning for any men reading this: Satan longs to keep you from being the spiritual leader the Lord deigns, desires, and directs you to be. He's out to do everything he can to keep you from influencing your wife and children, and, if you have any, your grandchildren for the Lord. Whatever else you do, you are the Lord's duly appointed and anointed spiritual leader, priest, and shepherd in your home, your family your flock as you serve him by influencing them.

Now, to any women reading this and growing nervous at this point, I am not suggesting a husband is the divinely designated dictator of a Christian family. He is neither the big boss of anybody nor is he superior to anyone, and he is not always right. His role does not include anything even close to an attitude of, "What I say goes, even if I'm wrong!" and, "It's my way or the highway!" Decisions of the home are not his alone. In a marriage, no husband should live and act independently of his wife. But what I am saying is that a husband answers to a God-ordained directive to be responsible for the spiritual life, health, and growth of his wife and children.

When the Apostle Paul said a husband should love his wife "just as Christ loved the church,"[54] meaning he was willing to die for her, he's saying the husband leads out of love, and his authority in spiritual matters is based on affection. A couple verses earlier, Paul calls the man "the *head* of the wife," but here he establishes

[53] Edwin Louis Cole, *Maximized Manhood* (Kensington, PA: Whitaker House 1982), 75. Cole was the founder of the Christian Men's Network.
[54] Ephesians 5:25.

that this role goes hand-in-hand with his being the spiritual *heart* of their life. A man never loves his wife more than when he prays for her.

I lost count of how many wives who, throughout my years as a local church pastor, asked me, "Why won't my husband be the spiritual leader in our home that he's supposed to be and we need him to be?" Based on my conversations, many women don't just want their husbands to live up to this role, they crave it! Whether they say it in so many words or not, their families look to the father for spiritual leadership.

Now, back to the men. Sir, when was the last time you read scripture with your family, or prayed with them, even prayed *for* them *in* their presence? Saying grace at meals doesn't count—it isn't enough—though I hear some guys can't even do that! Try this. From time to time, ask your wife, a child, or a grandchild, "Is there anything I can be praying about for you?" And when they tell you, start by praying with them right then and there.

A father had been praying for his young son and discussing biblical truth with him for several months. Unsure as to how he would lead his son to Christ should he have the opportunity, he began by asking the Lord to help him be prepared. One day a Christian magazine to which he subscribed arrived in the mail. That night, lying in bed reading it, an article titled "Leading a Child to Christ" got his attention. Just as he finished reading it, there was a soft knock at the bedroom door. "Come in," said dad. The door slowly swung open and in stepped his son with tears running down his face. "Dad," the boy said, "can I be saved without going down to the church and talking to the pastor?" His father, with the contents of the article fresh in his mind, reached for his Bible and had the privilege of leading his child to Christ. Now that's a dad prepared for and doing his job.

Pop, ask yourself this: "Do I know where every member of my family—wife, children, grandchildren—stands with the Lord? Or is where I stand with the Lord holding me back? Is there anything

I need to take care of first to be where I should be with the Lord, so I have the credibility in their eyes (and my own!) to be the spiritual leader in our home?"

No doubt much of the advice in this section seems impractical to some, including the single mom or the woman married to an unbelieving husband. In those cases, Christ still wants to be the head of the home, and women who find themselves in such circumstances are in the place to assume the role of spiritual responsibility. Old Testament precedent gives us the widowed Ruth's widowed mother-in-law, Naomi, and in another place, Queen Esther, as admirable examples. And in the New Testament, Paul's words to Timothy seem to indicate his grandmother and mother, Lois and Eunice, were in the same boat.

No matter who leads, however, there is a wonderful bonus that comes with bringing loved ones to the Lord in prayer. Ed Cole talked about that, and in doing so he made one of the most remarkable statements I have ever heard. I like it so much that in recent times I have written it in each new prayer journal at the start of the section of prayer concerns for my family. Cole said, "You become intimate with the one *to* whom you pray, the one *for* whom you pray, and the one *with* whom you pray."[55] Intimacy, a greater closeness to God and to each member of the family, is a by-product of fulfilling the intercessory calling on their behalf.

Praying It Forward

Thanks to a popular movie by the same title, the expression "pay it forward" has popularized the idea of responding to a kindness demonstrated to oneself by being kind to someone else. For instance, in recent years the practice of paying it forward takes place from time to time at the drive-through window of fast-food

---

[55] Cole, 77.

restaurants. Someone will place their order and then, when they pull forward to the pay window, pay not only for their meal but for the one being ordered by the car behind them. Most of the time, the person treating doesn't even know the person or persons in the car behind them, which adds to the fun of doing so. Sometimes it will continue for ten to fifteen cars!

There's the potential for something similar to happen in a realm much more important than hamburgers and fries. I call it, "*praying* it forward." Parents and grandparents can respond to the prayers invested in them by praying not only for their children and grandchildren, but for descendants beyond that they will never meet in this world. Praying for great-grandchildren, great-great-grandchildren, and beyond, to know, love, and serve the Lord. Some time ago I began doing that in personal prayer times as well as when Noni and I pray together.

In her book *Legacy of Prayer*, Jennifer Kennedy Dean draws on O. Hallesby's analogy of answers to prayer falling on us like a gentle rain, a rain that continues to fall on our dear ones to come even after we're in heaven. In doing so, we are establishing a spiritual trust fund for generations. Drawing upon her own family's experience, Dean writes:

> Our family has been a believing and praying family for three generations. The elders have prayed faithfully for their descendants. During my whole life I have walked in the prayers of my forebears and in the answers to these prayers. A quiet rain drips steadily upon me. I want my sons to walk in a gentle rain of answered prayers. I often tell them when they face decisions or

difficulties, "You are walking today in the answers to generations of prayers.[56]

What a wonderfully profound truth. Embrace it. Live it. And Dean goes on to remind us, prayer is not limited to linear time, because God isn't. He speaks of the past, present, and future as one. He is *I Am*, always in the present tense. "The answers to the prayers you pray today," she says, "will be answered in the lives of your descendants at the right time. Those answers will be working in their lives as if you had just prayed them." And then Dean makes this awe-inspiring, prayer-motivating observation: "Your prayers will put spiritual riches on deposit for them."

Proverbs 13:22 tells us, "Good people leave an inheritance to their grandchildren." Like many an aging parent and grandparent, my wife and I hope to do exactly what that verse praises. We hope whatever funds we have managed to save and invest will outlive us and pass on to our family as our financial legacy to them. Along with that, and even better, is the spiritual legacy we plan to pass on, not only to our children and grandchildren, but to generations of our descendants, as day by day we pray deposits into their spiritual trust fund.

Christian psychologist, author, and radio host James Dobson shares a fascinating story from his own family's history. It's worth quoting in its entirety:

> How can I explain the prayers of my great-grandfather (on my mother's side), who died the year before I was born? This wonderful man of God, G.W. McCluskey, took it upon himself to spend the hour between 11:00 A.M. and 12:00 noon every day in prayer specifically for the spiritual welfare of his family. He was talking to the Lord not only about

---

[56] Jennifer Kennedy Dean, *Legacy of Prayer* (Birmingham, AL: New Hope Publishers, 2002), 28–29.

those loved ones who were then alive. McCluskey was also praying for generations not yet born. This good man was talking to the Lord about me, even before I was conceived.

Toward the end of his life, my great-grandfather made a startling announcement. He said God had promised him that every member of four generations—both those living, and those not yet born—would be believers. Well, I represent the fourth generation down from his own, and it has worked out more interestingly than even he might have assumed.

The McCluskeys had two girls, one of whom was my grandmother and the other, my great-aunt. Both grew up and married ministers in the denomination of their father and mother. Between these women, five girls and one boy were born. One of them was my mother. All five of the girls married ministers in the denomination of their grandfather, and the boy became one. That brought it down to my generation. My cousin H.B. London and I were the first to go through college, and we were roommates. In the beginning of our sophomore year, he announced that God was calling him to preach. And I can assure you, I began to get very nervous about the family tradition!

I never felt God was asking me to be a minister, so I went to graduate school and became a psychologist. And yet, I have spent my professional life speaking, teaching, and writing about the importance of my faith in Jesus Christ. At times as I sit on a platform waiting to address a church filled with Christians, I wonder if my great-grandfather isn't smiling at me from somewhere. His prayers have reached across four generations of time to influence what I am doing with my life today.[57]

Remarkable story, isn't it? One more example of the power, purpose, and adventure of prayer, as well as of something we looked at in chapter one: Prayers are limitless and deathless.

Praying for Strangers

I'd like to expand the scope of this chapter and the verse that launched it and think about praying for those outside our personal and church families. I am talking about seizing the opportunity to bring people we barely know, or perhaps complete strangers, before the throne of grace. When a Facebook post details the need of someone we know little or even nothing about, a friend of a friend of a friend, we can click "like," perhaps add a comment, and then join hundreds, maybe thousands, responding to the same post and praying. A church email or phone chain sends out word of a member's relative in a far-off state rushed into emergency surgery. What an opportunity to join others interceding on behalf of someone we will likely never meet.

I remember reading in Frank Laubach's little book, *Prayer, the Mightiest Power in the World*, about how he would pray what he called "flash prayers." Passing someone on the street, sitting in a restaurant, riding on public transportation, or in some other setting, he would observe someone obviously hassled or hurting.

---

[57] James Dobson, *When God Doesn't Make Sense* (Carol Stream, IL: Tyndale House Publishers, 1993), 202–203.

Quickly and quietly, he would shoot up a flash prayer on their behalf. Often, he claimed, he immediately saw answers to his prayer as the subject of his praying settled down, smiled, and grew peaceful.

Our city's mayor wasn't exactly a stranger, but close to it. I had only spoken with her briefly at a couple community functions, so we were hardly best buds. Sensing the prompting of the Holy Spirit to go pray with her, I went to City Hall one day, walked into the mayor's office, introduced myself to the secretary, and asked if it might be possible for me to have a few minutes of the mayor's time. "Ten minutes tops," I promised.

She said she'd check with the mayor and returned to show me into her office. I had no idea what the mayor's beliefs were or weren't, but when I told her my purpose, she smiled and told me to proceed. I offered my prayer, shook her hand, thanked the secretary on my way out, and was gone. I can't say what ever became of that encounter, only that I know no prayer is ever wasted.

One of the most unusual experiences I have ever had of praying for a stranger occurred one time when Noni and I were enjoying a few days of vacation in Chicago. We had tickets for a musical but arrived in the theater's neighborhood too early to go in, so we went across the street to check out a large bookstore. We browsed awhile, each of us picked out a couple books to purchase, and I looked around for the place to pay. I spotted the checkout, tended by a young lady. Immediately, I sensed a gentle yet distinct prompting of the Spirit to pray with her.

When I told Noni, she said, "Do you want me to be with you?"

"No," I told her. "Why don't you stay here and pray no one interrupts, OK?"

After paying for our books, I said to the young woman, "I realize you don't know me from anybody, but I'm a follower of Jesus and I believe his Spirit has prompted me to pray with you. May I?"

Eagerly she responded, "Yes, please, if you would. I'd like that."

In a brief prayer I asked the Lord to bless her and to help her with any challenges she might currently be facing, ending by asking that he would be real to her, and that she would especially experience his love and grace. When I finished, she looked up, tears in her eyes, and said, "Thank you so much. You had no way of knowing, but this has probably been the worst day of my life." Now there were two of us with tears in our eyes. And not only had God heard *my* prayer, he'd heard another, Noni's, for in that crowded big city bookstore there were no interruptions while I was at the counter.

Praying with and for others is one of the reasons prayer is the adventure it is.

> Let us bathe ourselves, our family,
> and friends in prayer. Let us bathe
> our work and our enemies in prayer.
> And let us always come boldly to the
> throne of grace, that we may obtain
> mercy and find grace to help in time of need.
> —Jan Karon

SEVEN

The Hedge of God Encircling Us

Satan answered the Lord, "Does Job fear God for nothing? Haven't you placed a hedge around him, his household, and everything he owns?"

JOB 1:9–10[58]

Earlier I referred to one of my daughters, who a few years ago was enduring terrible hurt in the most difficult time of her life. One day a friend, a retired pastor who knew about her situation, said to me, "Have you thought of praying a hedge of protection around your daughter?"

"No, I haven't," I responded. "Over the years, I have prayed hedges around many people and yet not once have I thought of doing that for her. I shall take your words as a nudge from the Lord. Thank you."

The next day, I rose early and gave the entire morning to reading, thinking, and praying about what it means to pray a hedge of protection around someone. Never before had I been that analytical about it, but this time it hit closer to home than ever.

---

[58] Christian Standard Bible.

By noontime I was ready, and went to work, planting the hedge around my daughter.

By the way, during that same challenging time in our daughter's life, I felt prompted by the Spirit to assemble a team of intercessors to pray for her. Because of the biblical significance of the number, I contacted forty friends and relatives, asked them if they would take up the challenge, and then I kept them posted on developments. Thanks to "my forty faithful intercessors," as I called them, praying for a young woman surrounded by a hedge of protection, God intervened, and miraculously so.

Planting a Hedge of Protection

The biblical rationale for praying into place a protecting hedge is sketchy. For that reason, I can see where some might be uncomfortable with it. Only two brief statements in scripture refer to such a hedge. The primary reference, Job 1:9–10, records, "Satan answered the Lord, 'Does Job fear God for nothing? Haven't you placed a hedge around him, his household, and everything he owns.'"[59] Just because God placed a hedge around Job doesn't mean everyone can have one. Besides, no one that we know of, not even Job, prayed for the hedge. Apparently, at least as far as Satan was concerned, a sovereign God providentially put it into place. Yet in the Bible, God's protection is evident in many situations, assumed in other places, and prayed for in still others. The fact of divine protection, whether referred to as a hedge or not, is present throughout God's Word. At the very least, the idea of a surrounding hedge gives us a way to picture that protection, though personally I believe there's more to it than that.

The second reference to a protecting hedge in God's Word, Psalm 139:5, records David declaring to the Almighty, "You

---

[59] Christian Standard Bible.

have encircled me."[60] There are a variety of ways that has been translated: "You have surrounded me, enclosed me in, hemmed me in, and hedged me all around," to name a few. The point the psalm writer is making is that God is all around him to surround him, protecting him.

But why a hedge and not a wall? Scripture gives no definitive answer to that, but I like to think it's because a hedge is alive. A wall is erected and slowly wears down over time. The paint chips, the wood sustains water damage, the nails rust. If it's a stone wall, it eventually crumbles. A hedge, on the other hand, is a living, growing, rooted, and ever-thickening thing. When it is properly tended, it only grows bigger and stronger with time.

There is no biblical formula on how to plant a hedge, but I'll tell you how I like to do it. I start by praying in the name, by the power, and through the blood of Christ. Then I ask God to bind and banish Satan and his fellow fallen minions from the person for whom I am planting the hedge. Next, I state a Bible promise or some other scripture that relates to the person and the protection they need. Finally, I plant the hedge, literally praying and saying it into place with a few simple statements to that effect. But I'm not done with the hedge yet, not by a long shot.

People I know who have planted a hedge of protection around someone always stopped with the planting. But a hedge of protection, just like anything you plant in your yard, needs to be tended, cultivated, weeded, and watered if it's to remain healthy, strong, and growing. So, I regularly revisit the hedges I've planted for people and do some spiritual gardening.

My wife is the gardener of the family. While I have the gift of mowing a lawn, Noni is the skilled caretaker of all things growing, including her immense hosta garden, the envy of folks all around. I have told her we need to start charging admission for those who ask to tour it.

---

[60] Christian Standard Bible.

Noni invests hours of hard toil tending her plants, though it is clearly a labor of love. If she neglects them for even a little while, things start to go south in a hurry. So it is with a hedge you or I have planted around another person. It requires constant attention maintaining it.

As we have noted elsewhere in this book, real praying can be hard work, and that is especially true in this case. It takes discipline, time, effort, and just plain keeping at it to tend a hedge of God's protection you have planted around someone. Neglect it for long and it begins to lose its health and strength. As with Noni and her hostas, it may be hard work, but it is a labor of love.

Often when I tend a hedge, I begin with the following, word for word, and then elaborate with more prayer:

> Lord, please grow this hedge I have planted around [Name]. Grow it *higher* so the enemy can't climb over it. Grow it *wider* so the enemy can't see through it. Grow it *thicker* so the enemy can't get through it. Grow it *stronger* so the enemy can't destroy it. Grow it *deeper* so its roots sink into the soil of the Savior and grow it *thornier* for added protection. And if Satan does dare to mount an attack on this hedge, please confuse him in whatever he attempts.

There are all sorts of hedge-tending prayers you can offer, but the point is to keep praying until you are released from the burden. How do you know when that is? I like to apply an acronym I heard somewhere: "PUSH" (that is, Pray Until Something Happens). By "something," I mean an obvious answer comes, victory is achieved, the Lord lifts the burden, or he provides you with some other assurance. As we have seen more than once in this book, prevailing prayer is passionate, persistent prayer, and that's the kind with which we must PUSH.

Weaponizing Prayer

———

Planting a hedge of protection around others is just one way of doing what Franklin Graham calls "weaponizing prayer."[61] Praying the armor of God on yourself is another. With prayer in one hand and scripture in the other, we wield our two mightiest weapons in the power of the Holy Spirit whenever we enter the fray with our adversary, Satan, the deceiver of the believer. Never is it truer than in the realm of spiritual warfare that you're only as strong as your prayer life.

In Ephesians 6:10–18, Paul takes us into heaven's armory to outfit us for battle, but not before reminding us the Christian life is no walk in the park. It's lived out on a battleground, not a playground. It's all-out war and we'd better be combat ready. It's for real, not just a flesh-and-blood battle but a struggle with the spiritual forces of evil, a life-or-death fight to the finish against the powers of darkness in the devil's domain. If we are to stand strong when we are the target of an enemy tactic, we'd better have all our armor always on.

"Put on all of God's armor so that you will be able to stand firm against all strategies of the devil," the intrepid apostle instructs us. And the only way to put it on is to pray it on. Let me suggest just one way to approach such a prayer with something I prepared for my own use that is influenced by several "armoring-up" prayers I have liked and used over the years:

> Sovereign Lord God, bless me, your warrior, as I prepare for battle by dressing in the spiritual armor you have given to me to gain the victory over Satan's scams and schemes.
>
> I put on the belt of truth so I won't be a victim of Satan's lies and mind games, accusing me and

———

61 Franklin Graham, "Weaponizing Prayer," *Decision*, September 2019), 6–7.

trying to rob me of the joy and confidence of my salvation, that I might live in the powerful truth of *who* I am—a blood-bought, born-again believer for whom Christ died—and *whose* I am—a child of the Living God—my past forgiven, my present full and fortified, and my future forever with you.

And now I put on the breastplate of righteousness like a bullet-proof vest, protecting my heart from evil, leading to right living and obedience to you, my every thought and action guided, guarded, and governed by the Holy Spirit who fills me and the righteousness of Christ that covers me.

Next, I lace up and tie tight the shoes of peace, that I might have firm footing when I face the forces of darkness and march forward to share the gospel of light and life, grace and peace, with others.

And now I grip the shield of faith to deflect all the devil's blazing missiles of doubt, denial, and deceit, that I might not flag or fail in the face of fear, temptation, discouragement, or anything else he launches my way.

I place the helmet of salvation on my head, that I might keep my thinking fully and firmly focused on you, so Satan will establish no foothold in my thoughts and no stronghold in my mind.

With joy I pick up the inspired, authoritative, double-edged sword of the Spirit, the very Word of God, my only offensive weapon, that I might live in its truth and power and slash Satan's lies to pieces.

And now, Father, as I have put on the armor *in* prayer, help me to keep it well-oiled *with* prayer, through the mighty name of my matchless Lord, the conquering Christ. Amen.

God's SWAT Team

As Paul finishes cataloging the pieces of armor in Ephesians 6, he issues one of the Bible's signature calls to prayer, inviting us to enlist in what I call God's SWAT team (Spiritual Warfare Attack Team). Paul knows that even if you have all your armor always on, on the battlefields of spiritual warfare you're only as strong as your prayer life. Perhaps he was inspired by the example of Moses who, when the children of Israel took the battlefield against the Amalekites, stood on the mountain of prayer overlooking the valley of battle.[62] Paul's instructions are insightful and instructive:

> Pray in the Spirit at all times and on every occasion. Stay alert and be persistent in your prayers for all believers everywhere. And pray for me, too. Ask God to give me the right words so I can boldly explain God's mysterious plan that the Good News is for Jews and Gentiles alike. I am in chains now, still preaching this message as God's ambassador. So pray that I will keep on speaking boldly for him, as I should.[63]

---

[62] Exodus 17:8–13.
[63] Ephesians 6:18–29.

This call of Paul to weaponize prayer contains a sense of urgency as it tells us to pray "at all times and on every occasion." "Without ceasing" is how Paul puts it elsewhere in scripture. More than once he writes that he's praying "constantly." And in another place, he defines that as praying "night and day." And how does one pray without ceasing, constantly, night and day? Robert Morgan suggests it means we need to:

> Learn to employ all kinds of prayers—private prayer, corporate prayer, spontaneous prayer, morning prayer, evening prayer, prayers before meals, prayers before trips, walking prayers, written prayers, family prayers, church prayers, silent prayers, spoken prayers[64] ... To pray perpetually, to pray with great frequency and regularity, to pray at the drop of a hat, to pray during our regular times of intercession, but also to go around praying, as it were, under our breath.[65]

To hitchhike on Morgan's list of suggestions, we can "pray at all times and on every occasion" by taking it to the streets. I have friends who do prayer walks. Sometimes I like to pray when I'm out on a run, but I seem able to do that better when I am driving the car. That's when I use what I call "prayer triggers," locations around town that remind me to shoot up a prayer for someone or something whenever I drive past them. It's this Chicago-born, Italian guy's Christian version of a "drive by shooting." For instance, in the city where I live there is a missionary training college. Whenever I drive by it, I shoot up a prayer for the teachers, the students, and the ministries those students will someday have somewhere in the world.

---

[64] Morgan, "October 24," in *My All in All*.
[65] Morgan, "November 15."

I shoot up prayers for friends when I drive by their houses. Just one mile from our home lives a friend who battles a chronic illness. Many times, when I drive past her place, I pray for her. As I write this, we have good friends in our neighborhood who have had trouble selling their home. Since they are already in their new home, they are caught in the dreaded two-mortgage trap. I catch a glimpse of their home every time I drive into our development, and that's when I pray that in God's good timing he will open the door for it to sell.

The Christian elementary school our youngest grandchild, Brooke, attends, is just one and a half miles from our house. That's another "prayer trigger" of mine. Driving by I pray for the teachers, the principal, and all the staff. I pray for their protection and safety among other things.

Several times a week I drive past the street on which there used to live one of the most Christ-like persons I have ever known. Jennie Master has been in heaven several years now, but often when I pass her street, I thank God for the life she lived, the countless people she influenced for the Lord, and I ask him to help me be more Jennie-like so I will grow more Jesus-like.

Though he hit a few rough spots in his relationship with God, King David was prayer strong, an "at all times and on every occasion" man of prayer. Robert Morgan gives us just a sample of the many occasions that brought Israel's great shepherd, soldier, and sovereign to prayer:

> In Psalm 3, David prayed when endangered; in Psalm 4, before going to bed; in Psalm 5, before beginning the day; in Psalm 6, when guilty; in Psalm 7, when attacked; in Psalm 8, when impressed with creation's beauty; in Psalm 9, when happy; in Psalm 10, when God seemed far away.[66]

---

[66] Ibid., Morgan, October 24.

Unceasing prayer in the Spirit, then, along with the armor God gives us and the hedges planted around us, assure us of victory against our adversary, Satan.

> When a Christian shuns fellowship
> with other Christians, the devil smiles.
> When he stops reading the Bible,
> the devil laughs. When he stops
> praying, the devil shouts for joy.
> —Corrie Ten Boom

CONCLUSION

LTJ: Look to Jesus

As I come to the close of the final rewrite of my manuscript and prepare to send it back to the publisher, I find myself trembling, with tear-filled eyes, and with gratitude to God for his gift of prayer. I have found unwrapping that gift in these pages to be both a job and a joy. Hard work, yes, of course, but what joy has been mine to think of all prayer has meant and means to me. And as I prepare to dot the final *i* and cross the final *t*, it is with a yearning and commitment to appreciate the potential, practice the privilege, and experience more than ever the power of prayer. I am glad you and I travel together on our knees in this great adventure.

Renowned author Max Lucado imagines a scene in which Satan is seated in the back of a room where a dozen demons have come together to hear a report on their progress with one particularly stalwart saint.

"He won't stumble," groused the imp responsible for his demise. No matter what I do, he won't turn his back on God."

The council began to offer suggestions.

"Take his purity," one said.

"I tried," replied the fiend, "but he is too moral."

"Take his health," urged another.

"I did, but he refused to grumble or complain."

"Take his belongings."

"Are you kidding? I've stripped the man of every penny and possession. Yet he still rejoices."

For a few moments no one spoke. Finally, from the back of the room, came the low, measured voice of Satan himself. The entire council turned as the fallen angel rose to his feet. His pale face was all but hidden by the hood. A long cape covered his body. He raised his bony hand and made his point. "You must take what matters most."

"What is that?" asked the subordinate.

"You must take his prayer."[67]

Max Lucado imaginatively reminds us of a key theme of this book: You're only as strong as your prayer life.

For years I have signed-off on letters and emails with the initials "LTJ," standing for "Look to Jesus." It is inspired by Hebrews 12:2, which calls us to fix our eyes on Christ. People who know me well tend to identify those initials with me. And while my signature expression can be applied in more than one way, prayer, if it is anything, is looking to Jesus.

Look to Jesus and be prayer strong.

When you are tempted and tested and need to ponder His promises and claim his comfort, look to Jesus and pray. When you are downcast and discouraged and need to turn a *setback* into a *comeback*, look to Jesus.

When you are distressed and distraught over a culture that has swapped Christ the solid rock for a foundation and replaced it with the shifting sands of godlessness, look—I mean really look—to Jesus.

When you are tempted to forget he has promised to build his church and the gates of hell will not prevail against it, look to Jesus.

When everything going on around you leaves you overwhelmed and overcome, and it seems you can't cope, turn to Jesus in prayer, and he'll give you fresh hope.

When opportunities arise and possibilities abound, look to

---

[67] Max Lucado, *God Is With You Every Day* (Nashville, TN: Thomas Nelson, 2015, 2019), 150.

Jesus. Yes, in good times as well as bad, look to Jesus. Through sun and through storm, look to him. When the road is rough and the climb is steep, play it down and pray it up. When the debts are high and the funds are low, look to Jesus.

When you consider that your adversary the devil prowls about like a roaring lion, licking his chops and poised to pounce, you'd better look to Jesus. Pray.

When you're tempted to *let up* or *give up*, instead *look up*, to Jesus. Ask him to turn you around, turn you on, and turn you loose.

When you *gather* with others to worship on Sundays, then *scatter* from one another to *serve* on weekdays, look to Jesus. As you live, love, and labor for the Lord in worship, work, and witness, striving for faithfulness and fruitfulness, look to Jesus.

Go ahead, church of God, visionize, strategize, organize, mobilize, and evangelize, but first prioritize by looking to Jesus in prayer. Don't just pray God will bless your strategy. Remember, prayer is the *best* strategy.

When God sets before you an open door, look to Jesus. When you, as missionary William Carey so famously said, "Attempt great things *for* God and expect great things *from* God," pray. And then pray again. And then pray some more.

When God reveals his plans and unveils his purposes—when he brings new sight to your soul and new insight to you mind—look to Jesus. As he calls you higher, takes you deeper, and leads you further, pray.

Look to Jesus *in* everything, look to him *with* everything, look to him *for* everything and *through* everything. LTJ. Pray. After all, when it comes right down to it, you are only as strong as your prayer life. So, approach the throne of grace often and approach it boldly. There you will find mercy, grace, help, and hope, and you will get up off your knees prayer strong.

Look to Jesus as you strive and stretch toward the prayer life you've always wanted.

I'll close my conclusion as I began it—with the help of Max Lucado, who writes:

> Prayer is not a privilege for the pious, not the art of a chosen few. Prayer is simply a heartfelt conversation between God and his child. My friend, he wants to talk with you. Even now ... he taps at the door. Open it. Welcome him in. Let the conversation begin.[68]

My heart has heard you say, "Come and talk with me."
And my heart responds, "Lord, I am coming."
—Psalm 27:8

---

[68] Ibid., Lucado, 232.

MY DAILY PRAYER

Whatever else I converse with the Lord about on any given day, here is a prayer I created and use often at the close of my Bible and prayer time.

Lord, please help me to be yours, all yours, and nothing but yours today. Fulfill your plans and purposes for me. I want to keep in step with the Holy Spirit, so fill me fresh with his presence and power. May I be obedient to your Word, will, wisdom, instruction, and direction—always. When something is wrong in thought, word, or deed, may I conquer *it*, rather than let *it* conquer me. And when something is right, may I not hesitate to think, say, or do it. When I stumble and sin, help me to be quick to confess it, repent, and receive your forgiveness and grace. Yet, I would have all my armor always on, so I will ever be more than a conqueror. Fortify my faith and forge my future, for I want to live to your glory until you take me to Glory. This I pray in the matchless name of your Son, my Savior and faithful Friend, Jesus. Amen.

MY PRAYER FOR THE HURTING

Some days as I approach my prayer time, I find myself overwhelmed by the sheer number of my friends and relatives that are dealing with sickness, sorrow, despair, anxiety, fear, remorse, or regret. Some wrestle with emptiness, loneliness, bitterness, or brokenness. Others fight depression or some other form of mental illness. Most days I pray for them by name and by need. Often, I include the following prayer to help me scale that mountain of hurt.

O God who sees our hurts, carries our burdens, is attentive to our prayers, and supplies our every need; please be with the struggling, suffering, and sorrowing in my circle of family and friends this day. Deliver the distraught, comfort the brokenhearted, heal the physically afflicted, and strengthen the sorely tempted. Grant grace to the guilty, solace to the sorrowing, help to the helpless, and hope to the hopeless. Be merciful to those who are so anguished at heart and tormented of mind that they despair of even pressing on. May those who do not know you, look to you in repentance that they might experience the new birth, have a new life, and know the hope of heaven ahead. And please be near to those saints whose earthly sojourn is drawing to a close. On their bed of affliction may they know peace as they await the angel escort that even now is winging its way to guide them through death's dark valley and safely and eternally home. *Thus, I ask you to be merciful to all those on my heart today, showering them with your grace, filling them with your love, and giving them an unfaltering confidence in your unfailing presence that they might stand strong.* In the name of the one who bore our sins, carried our sorrows, and has promised to be with us always. Amen.

If you are interested in learning more about the author's Prayer Warrior Boot Camp as a possibility for your church, a retreat, or other event, or want to inquire about his availability to speak, please email him at thomasjramundo@gmail.com.